JOHN CALVIN ON PRAYER

EXPERIENCING AWE AND INTIMACY WITH GOD THROUGH THE POWER OF PRAYER

GODLIPRESS TEAM

CONTENTS

Introduction	vii
1. ENCOURAGEMENT TO PRAY	1
Daily Reflection	4
2. JESUS, OUR INTERCESSOR	6
Interceding for Others	8
Daily Reflection	8
3. HUMBLE PRAYER	10
Daily Reflection	13
4. THE LORD'S PRAYER (PART ONE)	15
Daily Reflection	18
5. THE LORD'S PRAYER (PART TWO)	20
Daily Reflection	23
6. THE LORD'S PRAYER (PART THREE)	25
Daily Reflection	29
7. ASK, SEEK, KNOCK	30
Daily Reflection	33
8. CHRIST, OUR MEDIATOR	35
Daily Reflection	37
9. A PRAYER OF FAITH	39
Daily Reflection	41
10. COMING TO THE THRONE	43
Daily Reflection	46
11. THE PHARISEE'S PRAYER	47
Daily Reflection	50
12. THE TAX COLLECTOR'S PRAYER	51
Daily Reflection	53

13. PRAYING IN CONFIDENCE	54
Daily Reflection	57
14. A PRAYER OF REPENTANCE	59
Daily Reflection	62
15. REJOICE AND PRAY	63
Daily Reflection	65
16. WHY WE PRAY	67
Why We Must Pray	68
Daily Reflection	70
17. PRAYING FOR FORGIVENESS	72
Daily Reflection	75
18. THANKSGIVING IN PRAYER	76
Daily Reflection	80
19. ALL OUR CARES TO HIM	81
Daily Reflection	85
20. PRAYING CONTINUOUSLY	86
Daily Reflection	89
21. PERSISTENCE IN PRAYER	90
Daily Reflection	92
22. A PRAYER OF HELP	94
Daily Reflection	97
23. WATCH AND PRAY	98
Daily Reflection	101
24. MARY'S PRAYER	103
Daily Reflection	106
25. HOW TO PRAY	108
Daily Reflection	111
26. THE HOLY SPIRIT'S HELP	112
Daily Reflection	115
27. PRAY IN THE SPIRIT	116
Daily Reflection	118

28. JESUS PRAYED	120
Daily Reflection	123
29. PRAYING PUBLICLY	124
Daily Reflection	127
30. DANIEL'S EXAMPLE (PART ONE)	129
Daily Reflection	133
31. DANIEL'S EXAMPLE (PART TWO)	134
Daily Reflection	137
About John Calvin	139
Bibliography	143

© **Copyright 2024 by GodliPress. All rights reserved.**

This book is copyright-protected. It is only for personal use. You cannot amend, distribute, sell, use, quote, or paraphrase any part of the content within this book without the express consent of the author or publisher, except in the case of brief quotations embodied in critical articles or reviews.

Scripture quotations are from The ESV® Bible (The Holy Bible, English Standard Version®), copyright © 2001 by Crossway, a Good News Publishers publishing ministry. Used by permission. All rights reserved.

INTRODUCTION

God asks us to pray because He wants us to commune with Him. He wants us to come to Him, to speak with Him, to bring Him our concerns, needs, desires, and joys. He is not an impersonal being in heaven that we need to appease like an idol, nor is He some type of Santa Claus who sits waiting to reward us with gifts if we've been good. He is an intimate God who desires to be as much in our lives as we need Him to be in ours. And prayer is the link that keeps that relationship personal.

Prayer is one of the keys to a fulfilled and powerful Christian life. There is no argument there. But how to go about it, why we do it, and who we pray to—this is where most of us trip and fall. We try different techniques, get confused, get frustrated when nothing happens, and often... we just give up, resigned to complaining or begging God when we're in a corner.

Our prayer lives become nothing more than an add-on, an extra chore we must accomplish because we are church goers, or something that makes us feel good in bad times.

And yet, it is one of the most crucial aspects of Christianity. It is the lifeline of our relationship with Jesus. We have the privilege of speaking with our Creator, our Savior, on a very personal level. It is a spiritual connection. This is why John Calvin focused on prayer in his acclaimed publication, *The Institutes of the Christian Religion*. Amongst other things, he tackled the concept of prayer, outlining its importance to us as Christians:

If we want to grow, we need to pray. And if we want to pray correctly, we need to understand who, what, why, and when.

With countless books by thousands of pastors and teachers, why would anyone need to delve back into the 16th century to find the answers? Who needs to dust off an ancient volume? Why not read something modern and up-to-date? Bookstores are overflowing with great titles, fresh ideas, and catchy covers. Not just for prayer, but for anything to do with Christianity. Surely, there's no need to dig up old passages.

And yet, these pages you are about to read are brimming with far more than most of those books put together. It's a bold, audacious statement to make, but there are enough reasons for promoting John Calvin above the plethora of modern-day writers.

For one, he knew what he was talking about. It's one of the reasons he is a pillar in church history. Standing up for truth against many false doctrines and heresies, his directives have remained as foundational instructions for any Christian, whether a pastor or a pew warmer.

Secondly, his insight into the Bible is astounding. Even his commentary on the Bible reveals a keen eye into the wisdom of God. By unpacking elements, verse by verse, Calvin's writings are not just good teachings or challenging ideas, they are solid and true!

Thirdly, there is an astounding wealth that comes from many of these men who wrote and preached during and after the Reformation. They were not just knowledgeable in the Scriptures, but they had to stake their lives on what they claimed and believed. Many Christians around that time faced martyrdom and were killed for their faith. Calvin's school of theology even came to be known as 'Calvin's school of death' due to the number of students who were subsequently put to death because of their witness for Christ.

Having stood the test of time and religious fanaticism, Calvin's words are not old and tired, they are tried and true. The only liberty we have taken is to modernize any out-of-date phrases and words. In no way have we dared alter the meaning or the heart of his teachings. Captured in these pages is a fresh look at his thoughts on prayer in today's English. We have carefully selected segments from his book, commentaries, lectures, and sermons that look at different facets of praying and how we can better come to terms with it for each of our lives.

Getting the Most Out of This Devotional

It's easy to read each chapter and walk away inspired, or even challenged to live better, pray more, and grow as a Christian. But just as James said, "Faith without works is dead" (James 2:26). If you never apply these principles and revelations to your life, then they remain nothing more than motivational prompts that will be forgotten over time. These daily reflections aim to take you a step further with a short recap and thought-provoking questions.

You can get the most out of these daily reflections by doing the following:

- **Be Personal**: These are not exam questions! Rather, view them as insights that provoke you to think further, especially how the concepts pertain to your life. This is the time for personal assessment.
- **Remain Flexible**: There is no order! But to help, we have set them in a month-long format, so you can read a chapter a day. This is purely to help you stay on track, but it is all up to you and your schedule. You can spend a few days reading just one chapter or all your time on one question and skip others. You can come back to them later. Use them as springboards to think about, meditate on, and study more.
- **Write Down**: Writing down thoughts and notes helps your brain store information, reinforcing what you learn. Make a note of other questions and other verses you think of. This method also serves as a

record so you can look back on your answers and see what needs attention and work so you can grow in faith.
- **Search Deeper:** All these teachings are rooted in the Word of God, so it helps if you have your Bible close. Look up the verses, find any other related scriptures, and examine each statement to ensure they are of sound doctrine. It's also a wonderful way of studying what the Bible has to say. As incredible as Calvin's words are to help you, nothing compares with the truth of God's Word for guidance and growth.

Our hope is that through Calvin's perceptions, you will grow as a Christian, realize the powerful means we have of communicating with our Lord Jesus, and draw closer to Him more and more.

1

ENCOURAGEMENT TO PRAY

First of all, then, I urge that supplications, prayers, intercessions, and thanksgivings be made for all people, for kings and all who are in high positions, that we may live a peaceful and quiet life, godly and dignified in every way.... I desire then that in every place the men should pray, lifting holy hands without anger or quarreling.
—1 Tim. 2:1-3, 8

"First of all, then, I urge that supplications, prayers, intercessions."

Paul says that whenever public prayers are offered, petitions and supplications should be made for all men, even for those who are not at all related to us. He joins three terms together to encourage and urge us toward sincere and constant prayer. We know how lazy we are in this duty and therefore, we need the Holy Spirit to encourage us.

"And thanksgivings be made for all people."

He calls us to make supplication to God for the salvation of unbelievers and also to give thanks for their prosperity and success. That wonderful goodness which He shows every day, when "he makes his sun rise on the evil and on the good, and sends rain on the just and on the unjust" (Matt. 5:45), is worthy of being praised; and our love for our neighbor should extend to those who are unworthy of it.

"For kings and all who are in high positions."

He specifically mentions kings and others in power because at that time they were sworn enemies of Christ. Therefore, we might think that we should not pray for those who devote all their power and wealth to fight against the kingdom of Christ. Paul solves this problem by explicitly encouraging Christians to pray for them, as well. The wickedness of people is not a reason why God's order to love should not be followed. Since God appointed magistrates and heads of state to oversee and preserve people, however badly they do their jobs, we should not stop loving what belongs to God, and to desire that it will remain in place.

That is why believers, in whatever country they live in, must not only obey the laws and the government but also in their prayers supplicate God for their salvation. Jeremiah said to the Israelites, "Pray to the Lord on [Babylon's] behalf, for in its welfare you will find your welfare" (Jer. 29:7). The universal doctrine is that we should desire peace for those governments which have been appointed by God.

"That we may lead a peaceful and quiet life."

By showing the advantage, he gives extra encouragement in the fruits we reap from a well-regulated government. The first is a peaceful life; for magistrates are armed with the sword to keep us in peace. If they did not restrain wicked men, every place would be full of robberies and murders. The true way of maintaining peace, therefore, is, when everyone gets what they deserve, and the violence of the more powerful is kept under control.

"Godly and dignified in every way."

The second fruit is the preservation of godliness when magistrates promote religion to uphold the worship of God, and to take care that sacred laws are observed and respected. The third fruit is public decency because it is also the business of magistrates to prevent people from becoming immoral. If these three things are taken away, what will the condition of human life be?

"I desire then that in every place the men should pray."

We need "the Spirit of adoption," for us to call on God in the right way. This is the same phrase used in the beginning of 1 Corinthians, "with all those who in every place call upon the name of our Lord Jesus Christ" (1 Cor. 1:2), so there is now no difference between Gentile, Jew, Greek, or other, because we all have God as our Father; and in Jesus the prophecy of Malachi comes true, that not only in Judea, but throughout the whole world, pure sacrifices are offered (Malachi 1:11).

"Lifting holy hands without anger or quarreling."

This is the expression of a pure heart. When we ask God, we look up, and this attitude is linked with true godliness, provided we are seeking God in heaven. While we should pray with a peaceful conscience and assured confidence, some think that the apostle here demands that our minds should be calm and free from all uneasy feelings toward God and people, because there is nothing that blocks prayer more than quarrels and strife. Jesus said that if anyone has a dispute with his brother, they should go and be reconciled before offering a gift on the altar.

Daily Reflection

These daily reflections are simply summaries with a few extra thoughts on what Calvin writes about prayer. They are to personalize the concepts and ideas to bring them closer to home so you can apply them to your own life. This is how we grow, by applying biblical doctrine to our everyday walk with God.

Paul sees the need to encourage us in prayer because we often get lazy or confused in coming to God. He sets out some parameters and expectations for us if we are to pray correctly. It is not so much a strict code as it is an encouragement. We all lose our way in prayer sometimes—our minds wander, our hearts are just not in it, or we have no words or thoughts. Paul knows this, and so he urges all Christians in this exercise of faith.

1. What is the difference between *"supplications, prayers, intercessions"*? Look them up in the dictionary or other Bible translations to understand their meanings.

2. What is the significance of thanking God for other people? Do you ever do this?
3. It's interesting that Jeremiah insists the people pray for the government, even though it was not a godly one. What do you think about this?
4. Why is a "pure heart" so important in prayer?

2

JESUS, OUR INTERCESSOR

*Christ Jesus is the one who died—more than that, who was raised—
who is at the right hand of God, who indeed is interceding for us.*
—Rom. 8:34

Jesus told His disciples that they would have access to Him through prayer after He ascended to heaven: "In that day you will ask in my name" (John 16:26).

Under the Law, anyone who prayed was only heard through a mediator because no one but the priest could enter the sanctuary (Exod. 28:9-21). The rest of the people had to stand in the outer court since the sacrifice was enough to approve and confirm their prayers. The Law taught that everyone was excluded from the face of God. Therefore, we needed a Mediator to stand in our name and carry us on His shoulders, that we may be heard through Him. The Law also taught that our prayers would never be acceptable unless they are washed by

His blood. Anyone who wanted to receive something put all their hopes on sacrifices because they knew that by sacrifice all prayers were approved: "Remember all your offerings," says David, "and regard with favor your burnt sacrifices!" (Ps. 20:3).

So, when God receives the prayers of His people, He is appeased right from the start by the intercession of Jesus.

Why then does Jesus speak of a new period (*"in that day"*) when the disciples were to begin praying in His name, unless we understand and see it in grace? This is why He also said, "Until now you have asked nothing in my name. Ask, and you will receive, that your joy may be full" (John 16:24). Not that they were completely ignorant about the role of Mediator (all the Jews grew up learning about its function), but they did not clearly understand that Jesus, by going to heaven, would be the advocate of the church more than before. Therefore, to encourage them when he left, He confirmed His role of advocate. While they had not been able to enjoy this benefit before, through His intercession they would be able to call on God with more freedom.

This is why Paul says we have "confidence to enter the holy places by the blood of Jesus, by the new and living way that he opened for us" (Heb. 10:19-20). Since He is the only way and the only access we have to draw near to God (John 14:6), those who deviate from this way and decline this access have no other options. For anyone who rejects Jesus as Mediator, God's throne offers nothing but judgment and terror. As the Father has consecrated Him (John 6:27) our Guide (1 Cor. 11:3; Eph. 1:22, 4:15, 5:23; Col. 1:18) and Head (Matt. 2:6), those who abandon or turn aside from Him in any way, dishonor and remove the authority God has given Jesus.

Interceding for Others

Christ is the only Mediator whose intercession turns the Father's ear and makes Him approachable (1 Tim. 2:5). Even though Christians can intercede on behalf of other people and ask God for their salvation (Eph. 6:18-19; 1 Tim. 2:1), these prayers still depend on that one intercession. Our prayers for others that we offer up as one body in the church come from love for one another, but they still flow from the head of the body—Jesus. And since our prayers are said in His name, this clearly shows that none of us can gain anything from any prayers without the intercession of Christ.

There is nothing in the intercession of Christ that prevents Christians in the church from praying for each other, so it is acceptable as long as all those intercessions made in the church come under that one intercession.

This should make us especially grateful, that God, pardoning our unworthiness, not only allows each person to pray for themselves but also allows everyone to intercede for each other as part of the body.

Daily Reflection

Jesus' intercession is integral to our prayer lives. Without it, we would have no access to the Father. Calvin opens up this concept by backing it up with a host of verses to show us how this works in our favor. If you have never considered the importance of Jesus' role, it should start to become clearer after this chapter. It is a very interesting topic that is often overlooked by many Christians and robs them of understanding prayer in its entirety. Knowing He not only paid for our salvation but opens the way for our prayers to rise up to God is an incredible insight that enriches any Christian's communication with the Father.

1. Why is it important that Jesus intercedes for us?
2. How does this link with the Old Testament requirements for prayers and offerings?
3. How does it change your prayer knowing you can receive nothing except through Jesus?

3

HUMBLE PRAYER

And when you pray, you must not be like the hypocrites...But when you pray, go into your room and shut the door and pray to your Father who is in secret. And your Father who sees in secret will reward you. And when you pray, do not heap up empty phrases as the Gentiles do, for they think they will be heard for their many words. Do not be like them, for your Father knows what you need before you ask Him.
—Matt.6:5-7

"*And when you pray.*"

Jesus gives the same instruction to prayer as the one he gave for tithing. It is disrespectful when hypocrites pray in public to receive glory from people, or at least pretend to pray. But since hypocrisy is always ambitious, it is not surprising that it is also blind. Therefore, Jesus says that if His disciples want to pray correctly, they must *"go into your room and shut the door."*

Some say this is a metaphor referring to the inner places of the heart, but there is no truth to this belief. We are commanded, in many verses, to pray to God or to praise him, in public, surrounded by people, and before everyone. This is for the purpose of testifying our faith or gratitude, and also to motivate others through our example to do the same. Jesus commands us to always focus on God when we engage in prayer.

"Go into your room and shut the door."

We must not literally interpret these words as if He ordered us to avoid people or that we are only praying correctly when there are no witnesses. He meant that we should seek seclusion rather than desire a crowd of people to see us praying. It is an advantage for us to be able to pour out prayers and groans before God with more freedom without others watching. Being on our own also helps our minds to be free and disengaged from all distracting thoughts, which is why Jesus often chose quiet, secluded spots for the sake of prayer.

But the main reason for this command is to stop pride in prayer. If someone prays alone or in the presence of others, they should have the same feelings as if they were shut up in their room and had no other witness but God. When Jesus says, *"Your Father who sees in secret will reward you,"* He simply says that the reward is not paid as a debt but is a free gift.

"Do not heap up empty phrases."

He criticizes the fault of having too many words in prayer. There are two words used, but in the same sense: "an unnecessary and exaggerated repetition," and "useless talk." Jesus rebukes those who think they can persuade and beg God by pouring out lots of words. This is consistent throughout the Bible when talking about sincerity in prayer—when prayer is offered with sincerity, the mouth does not go before the heart. You cannot get the grace of God by a meaningless flow of words, only a devout heart can throw out its emotions like arrows, to pierce heaven.

Religious people think that the more words they mutter, the more diligently they have prayed. They think long and tedious chanting soothes the ears of God, so it continually resounds in their cathedrals. However, Jesus condemns the belief that people can find favor with God because of their long murmurings.

"Your Father knows."

This single remedy is sufficient for removing and destroying this false belief. How can we think we are gaining any advantage when we bore God with many words because we think that He is like us, a person who needs to be informed and solicited? If we know that God not only cares for us, but knows all our wants, and anticipates our wishes and anxieties before we have stated them, we will leave useless repetitions and will pray long enough that our faith has been engaged. It is ridiculous to approach God with rhetorical exaggerations, in the expectation that He will be moved by an abundance of words.

But if God knows what we need before we ask Him, what is the advantage of prayer? If He is ready, of His own free will, to help us, what is the purpose of our prayers that interrupt His provision? The design of prayer gives an easy answer. Believers do not pray to inform God about things He does not know or to motivate Him to do His duty as though He is reluctant. Instead, we pray so that we can motivate ourselves to seek Him, exercise our faith in meditating on His promises, and relieve ourselves from our anxieties by pouring them onto Him. Prayer exists so we can declare that only from Him do we hope and expect all good things for ourselves and for others.

God has decided, without being asked, to give us blessings, but He also promises that He will grant them to our prayers. We must, therefore, hold onto both of these truths, that He freely anticipates our wishes, and yet that we receive what we ask by prayer.

Daily Reflection

This idea of secret prayer has been misread or taught incorrectly in some instances. Instead of physically shutting yourself off, it is talking more about a state of heart, an attitude. While it is very beneficial to close yourself off from distractions and noise while communing with God, it is not always possible to find a quiet place. Here, Calvin alludes to the idea that it has more to do with whether we are looking for praise from others than praise from our Father. If God is our only audience, then we should have no pretense or hypocritical intentions.

1. Do you have a room or quiet place where you can pray? Does it help you?

2. How do you deal with distractions in your prayer time?
3. Why do you think pride in prayer is such a big obstacle for so many Christians?
4. Have you ever used big words or phrases in prayer and thought that they sounded really good or convincing to others and possibly God as well?
5. Why is God not moved by these kinds of prayers?

4

THE LORD'S PRAYER (PART ONE)

Pray then like this: Our Father in heaven, hallowed be your name, your kingdom come, your will be done, on Earth as it is in heaven.
—Matt. 6:9-10

Jesus does not want us to pray in a structured form of words but points out what the object of all our wishes and prayers should be. But often when we pray, our senses fail us. No one can pray correctly unless their lips and hearts are directed by the heavenly Master. That is why this rule of prayer was given, to frame our prayers so they will be approved by God. It was not Jesus' intention to prescribe the dictated words we must use.

"Our Father in heaven."

Whenever we pray, there are two things to think about for us to have access to God and rely on Him with complete confidence: His fatherly love toward us and His unlimited power.

We must not doubt that God is willing to receive us and is ready to listen to our prayers. He has been given the title of Father, so we have enough reason to be confident in Him. But this is only half of it because by saying He is *"in heaven,"* it means everything is subject to Him—the world, and everything in it, is held by His hand—as David says, "He who sits in the heavens laughs" (Ps. 2:4), and, "Our God is in the heavens; he does all that he pleases" (Ps. 115:3).

When it says God is in heaven, it does not mean He just lives there, but as the Bible says: "Even highest heaven, cannot contain him" (2 Chron. 2:6). This separates Him from being on the same level as creatures and reminds us He is higher than the whole world. At the beginning of the prayer, Jesus wanted His own people to have confidence in the goodness and power of God, because unless our prayers are established on faith, they have no advantage. We cannot call God our Father except through our union to the body of Christ where we are acknowledged as His children. Then there is also no other way of praying correctly except by approaching God through a Mediator.

"Hallowed be your name."

The first three petitions take our eyes off ourselves to seek the glory of God. It is not separate from our salvation, but the majesty of God should be preferred to everything else on our minds. It is an incredible advantage to us that God reigns and receives the honor due to Him. We cannot properly promote the glory of God unless we forget ourselves and lift our minds to seek His greatness. There is a close connection between these three petitions. The sanctification of the name of God is always connected with His kingdom, and the most important part of his kingdom lies in His will being done.

This petition is so the glory of God will shine in the world and be acknowledged by us. The faith we give to the word of God is how we put a "seal to this, that God is true" (John 3:33).

"Your kingdom come."

We must first look at the definition of the kingdom of God. He reigns among us when we voluntarily devote and submit ourselves to be governed by Him, placing our bodies under His rule and renouncing our desires. Our emotions are like many soldiers of Satan that oppose the justice of God and block His reign. By this prayer, we ask that He remove all obstacles and bring us all under His rule and lead us to meditate on life in heaven.

This is done partly by the preaching the word and partly by the secret power of the Spirit. It is His will to govern people by His word. Both the word and Spirit must be joined together so the kingdom of God may be established. That is why we pray that God would bring His power, both by the word and by the Spirit, so that the whole world will submit to Him. The kingdom of God is opposed to all disorder and confusion, so the beginning of the reign of God in us is the destruction of the old man and the denial of ourselves so that we may be renewed to another life.

There is another way God reigns: When He overthrows His enemies and forces them to surrender to His authority, "until his enemies should be made a footstool for his feet" (Heb.

10:13.) The main part of this prayer is that God would enlighten the world by the light of His word—to form the hearts of people by His Spirit for them to obey His justice, and to restore order in the world by His power. As the kingdom of God is continually growing and advancing in the world, we must pray every day that it will come. No matter how much sin there is in the world, the same amount of the kingdom of God, which brings perfect righteousness, is still coming.

"Your will be done."

Although the will of God is simple, it is shown to us in the Bible in a double aspect. We are commanded to pray that His will may be done—that all creatures obey Him without opposition, and without reluctance. This is made clear by comparing *"on earth"* with *"as it is in heaven."* Just as His angels are always ready to carry out His commands (Ps. 103:20), so we desire that everyone might have their will molded in harmony with the righteousness of God, that they may freely bend in whatever direction He chooses. It is a holy desire when we bow to the will of God and submit to His appointments. But this prayer implies something more. It is a prayer that God will remove all the stubbornness of people who rise in rebellion against Him and make them gentle and submissive so that they will desire nothing except what pleases Him.

Daily Reflection

The Lord's Prayer is the most famous version of a prayer, often used at funerals, gatherings, services, and certain churches. Many people have heard (and said) it so many times that it has become more of a rote invocation than a heartfelt communication with God. This can be said for many of our own prayers that are like dead words spoken to the air instead of a spiritual connection. However, when we take a fresh look at the words and their meaning, an old dusty rendition can have new life breathed into it.

1. Where did you last say the Lord's Prayer? Did it have any meaning for you?
2. Why do you think this prayer is used so often?
3. Why does the prayer start with declaring that our Father is in heaven?
4. What is the significance of these first three petitions?
5. Do you ever pray for God's kingdom and will in your own life?

5

THE LORD'S PRAYER (PART TWO)

Give us this day our daily bread. —Matt. 6:11

In the first three petitions, Jesus instructs us to seek the glory of God and then points out, in the second part, what we should ask for ourselves. The prayers which we offer for our salvation or for our own advantage should always give the first place to the glory of God.

Though the forgiveness of sins is preferred to food because the soul is more valuable than the body, Jesus began these petitions with bread and the needs of earthly life so we might later raise our focus from that point. We do not ask that our daily bread is given to us before asking to be reconciled to God as if food for the stomach is more valuable than the eternal salvation of the soul, but we do so that we may ascend by steps from earth to heaven. Since God nourishes our bodies, there is no doubt that He is much more concerned with our spiritual life. This kind way of treating us lifts our confidence higher.

Some people think that daily bread means supernatural bread. This is ridiculous. They say that when we are in the presence of God, Jesus would not tell us to speak about natural food. But we find this kind of instruction all through the Bible, to lead us to expect heavenly blessings by giving us a taste of physical blessings. It is the true proof of our faith when we ask for everything from God, and not only acknowledge Him to be the only fountain of all blessings but feel that his fatherly kindness extends to the smallest matters, to even take care of our bodies.

Jesus speaks here of physical food, otherwise the prayer would be defective and incomplete. We are told in many verses to throw all our cares onto God, and He graciously promises, that "no good thing does he withhold from those who walk uprightly" (Ps. 84:11). In a perfect rule of prayer, some direction must be laid down for all the needs of our lives. Besides, the word *"daily"* means that we must ask God only what is necessary for the day. There is no doubt He intended to restrain and guide our desire for earthly food, on which we are all dependent. The word *"bread"* has a greater meaning because we do not only ask that God will supply us with food, but that we may receive all that is necessary for our lives.

The meaning is now obvious. We are first commanded to pray that God would protect the life which He has given to us in the world and that He would supply us with everything He knows we need. As the kindness of God flows uninterrupted to feed us, the bread He gives is continual. This means we pray in this way: "O Lord, since our life needs every day new supplies, please give them to us without interruption." The adverb *"daily"* is added to restrain our excessive desire, and to teach us that we depend on the kindness of God for every moment and should be content with how much He gives us "from day to day."

Jesus has given a rule for prayer that applies to all Christians. Some people are rich and have their annual produce already stored up. Why does He command them to ask what they already have at home, and to ask every day those things they have an abundant supply of? The reply is easy. These words remind us that unless God feeds us daily, the largest accumulation of the necessities of life will be useless. Even if we have an abundance of food and drink, and everything else, unless they are watered by the secret blessing of God, they will suddenly vanish, or we will not be able to access them, or they will lose their natural power to support us, so that we will starve surrounded by plenty. So, there is no reason to wonder if Jesus invites both the rich and poor to apply to their Heavenly Father for all their needs. No one will sincerely offer a prayer like this unless they have learned by Paul's example of "facing plenty and hunger, abundance and need" (Phil. 4:12), to endure patiently in poverty or his humble condition and not to be misled by a false confidence in his abundance.

Do you wonder why we ask for bread to be given to us when it is called *"our"* bread? It is not because it belongs to us by right, but because the fatherly kindness of God has set it apart for our use. It becomes ours because our Father freely gives it to us since we need it. The fields must be cultivated, the harvest must be collected, and every person must do the work they are called to do for food to be acquired. But this does not stop us from being fed by the undeserved kindness of God, without which we would waste work with nothing to show for it. So, we are taught that what we have acquired by our own work is His gift. If we want God to feed us, we must not take what belongs to others. Everyone who is taught by God (John 6:45), whenever they pray this prayer, makes a declaration that they desire nothing except what is theirs.

Daily Reflection

By focusing a whole section on this aspect of the Lord's Prayer, Calvin manages to teach us the notion of asking God for our daily needs. Sometimes we are too busy asking for things we want or for Him to get us out of situations. We forget that He is our provider, not just of miracles and help in times of trouble, but right down to the most simple things like bread. Our prayers become grounded and real when we bring them back to basics—relying on our Father for every single thing we need to survive. It is a humbling but very good place to pray from.

1. Does the request for daily bread have anything to do with saying "grace" before meals? Do you think this is necessary for us as Christians?
2. What would you define as daily bread?

3. Is there a difference in the prayers of the rich and the poor?
4. Why does Calvin emphasize the "*our*" bread in this part? What does it mean for us in our prayers?

6

THE LORD'S PRAYER (PART THREE)

And forgive us our debts, as we also have forgiven our debtors, and lead us not into temptation, but deliver us from evil.
—Matt. 6:12-13

"*And forgive us our debts.*"

Even though Jesus said the Lord's prayer in a certain form, He did not intend for us to stick to it all in that order. It is written so that our prayers do not become a wall that blocks our approach to God (Isa. 59:2) or a cloud that prevents Him from engaging with us (Isa. 44:22) or so He "wrapped [Himself] with a cloud so that no prayer can pass through" (Lam. 3:44).

So, we should always begin with the forgiveness of sins, because the first hope of being heard by God is when we have His favor. There is no way He is *"pacified toward thee"* (Ezek. 16:63 KJV) but by forgiving our sins. Jesus included everything that related to the eternal salvation of the soul and to the spiritual life in two petitions because these are the two leading points of the divine covenant our salvation consists of. He offers us a free reconciliation by "not counting their trespasses against" us (2 Cor. 5:19) and promises the Spirit to write the righteousness of the law on our hearts.

In Matthew, sins are called debts, because they expose us to condemnation from God, and make us debtors—they alienate us entirely from God so that there is no hope of having peace and favor except by forgiveness. Paul tells us that "all have sinned and fall short of the glory of God" (Rom. 3:23) and "that every mouth may be stopped, and the whole world may be held accountable to God" (Rom. 3:19).

Even though the righteousness of God shines in Christians, as long as they are surrounded by the flesh, they are under the burden of sins. No one will become pure if they have no need for the mercy of God, and if we want it, we must feel our wretchedness. Anyone who dreams of only being perfect in this world, to be free from every spot and blemish, not only ignores their sins but renounces Jesus, because they are not a part of His church. When He commands all His disciples to come to Him daily for the forgiveness of sins, everyone who thinks that they have no need of such a remedy is not one of those disciples.

The forgiveness we ask for is not the same that the world tries to buy for its own deliverance. A creditor does not forgive if he has received payment and asks for nothing more —but someone who willingly and generously departs from his just claim, and frees the debtor, forgives. God does not forgive or pardon except by removing the condemnation that they deserve.

"As we also have forgiven our debtors."

This condition is added so no one can presume to approach God and ask forgiveness who is not pure and free from all resentment. And yet, the forgiveness that we ask God to give us does not depend on the forgiveness we give to others. Jesus was encouraging us to forgive the offenses which have been committed against us. He wanted to remind us of the feelings which we should have toward other Christians when we desire to be reconciled to God. If the Spirit of God reigns in our hearts, all bad feelings and revenge should be removed. The Spirit is the witness of our adoption (Rom. 8:16), and this is put down as a mark to distinguish the children of God from strangers. "Debtors" is used here, not for those who owe us money, or any other service, but to those who are indebted to us on account of offenses which they have committed.

"And lead us not into temptation."

Some people have split this petition into two. This is wrong because the nature of the subject shows it is one and the same petition. The use of the word *"but,"* connects the two clauses together. We can read the sentence: So, we may not be led into temptation, deliver us from evil. The meaning is: "We are aware of our own weakness, and want to enjoy the protection of God, that we may remain secure against all the assaults of Satan." From the previous petition, we saw that no one can be a Christian if they do not acknowledge themselves to be a sinner. Whoever asks for the assistance of God to overcome temptations, acknowledges that, unless God delivers them, they will be constantly falling.

The word *"temptation"* is often used generally for any kind of trial, but here, it means inward temptation—the scourge of the devil—because it excites our lust. It would be silly to ask God to keep us free from everything that is a trial of our faith. It is not impossible for us to feel such pricks in our minds (we have a constant warfare with the flesh), yet we ask the Lord not to let us be thrown down, or be overwhelmed, by temptations.

We will constantly stumble and fall if God does not uphold us with His hand, so Jesus used this phrase: *"Lead us not into temptation,"* or in another translation, "Bring us not into temptation." James tells us that "each person is tempted when he is lured and enticed by his own desire" (James 1:14), but God does not just hand us over to the will of Satan to kindle the flame of lust, but uses him as the agent of His judgment, when He chooses to drive people straight to destruction. In the same sense, we read of Saul where "a harmful spirit from the Lord" is said to have "tormented him" (1 Sam. 16:14). And yet, we will not say God is the author of evil, because, by giving people over "to a debased mind" (Rom. 1:28), He does not exercise a confused tyranny, but executes His just judgments.

"But deliver us from evil."

The word "evil" can either mean an evil thing or the evil one, or it can refer to sin. The meaning remains the same: we are in danger from the devil and from sin if the Lord does not protect and deliver us.

Daily Reflection

Picking apart the Lord's Prayer can help us see the wisdom of Jesus when he taught this outline to his disciples. It was not so much a format to be repeated, but rather a way of ordering our own praises, thanksgiving, requests, and confessions. Although the words are important in their meaning, they are only a blueprint for our own words, and our own hearts to pour out to God.

1. What do you understand by the word *"debts"*?
2. Why is forgiveness such an important part of our prayers?
3. Why do we need to pray to not be led into temptation? Read James 1:13-15 and 1 Corinthians 10:13.
4. Has your view of the Lord's prayer changed after reading these three chapters? How?

7

ASK, SEEK, KNOCK

Ask, and it will be given to you; seek, and you will find; knock, and it will be opened to you. For everyone who asks receives, and the one who seeks finds, and to the one who knocks it will be opened... Your Father who is in heaven give[s] good things.
—Matt. 7:7-8, 11

"*Ask, and it will be given to you.*"

This is a call to prayer, and although it should be our first concern, we are so careless and lazy. Jesus emphasizes the same thing in three different ways. There is no complicated language when he says, "Ask, seek, knock," but because it is such a simple doctrine, He continues to motivate us. It is the same with the promises that are added: "*You will find,*" "*it will be given to you,*" and "*it will be opened to you.*" Nothing is better for motivating us to prayer than a full conviction that we will be heard. Those who doubt can only pray without real interest, and prayer, without faith, is a worthless act. So, Jesus not only tells us what we should do, but He promises that our prayers will not be fruitless.

First, we learn that this rule of prayer is given to us, so we can be fully convinced that God will be gracious to us and will listen to our requests. Also, whenever we pray, or whenever we feel that our efforts in prayer are not enough, we should remember the gentle assurance Jesus gives us of God's fatherly kindness. All of us, trusting the grace of Jesus, will gain confidence in prayer and will be able to call on God "in Christ Jesus our Lord, in whom we have boldness and access with confidence through our faith in him" (Eph. 3:11-12).

But, because we are so slow to trust Jesus, the promise is repeated in different words. He uses the metaphor "seek," because we think our wants and necessities are far from us—and "knock," because our natural senses imagine those things which are not instantly received are closed off.

"For everyone who asks receives."

Jesus presents the grace of His Father to those who pray. He tells us God is prepared to listen to us if we pray to Him, and His riches are at our command if we ask for them. These words mean that those who do not have what they need and do not use this method to overcome their poverty, get what they deserve for their laziness. When believers are asleep, God guards their salvation and anticipates their wishes. Nothing could be worse if God waited for our prayers or took no notice of us because of our carelessness or stupidity. He is the one who gives us faith, which goes before every prayer.

But in the same way, Jesus talks to His disciples, He reminds us how pleased our heavenly Father is to give us His gifts. Even though He gives all things freely to us, to exercise our faith, He commands us to pray so He can give us those blessings which flow from His undeserved goodness.

Verse 9 is a comparison where Jesus contrasts the selfishness of people with the unlimited goodness of God. Self-love makes us malicious, because every person is too devoted to themselves, and neglects and disregards others. But this weakness gives way to the stronger feelings of a father's love so that people forget themselves and give to their children with overflowing freedom. This only happens because God, of whom the whole family in heaven and earth originates (Eph. 3:15), drops into their hearts some of His goodness. If the little drops produce such an amount of generosity, what should we expect from the inexhaustible ocean? Would God, who opens the hearts of people, shut His own? Let us also remember that verse in Isaiah: "A woman forget her nursing child" (Isa. 49:15), but the Lord will always be a Father to us.

"Your Father who is in heaven give[s] good things."

Jesus mentions this so the believers will not have silly or unacceptable desires in prayer. We know how much our flesh influences us, and we do not hold back when we ask from God. If He does not humor our foolishness, we shout at Him. So, Jesus encourages us to submit our desires to the will of God, so He can give us only what He knows is good for us. We must not think that he takes no notice of us when He does not answer our wishes, because He has a right to decide what we actually need. When all our emotions blind us, the rule of prayer must come from the Word of God because we are not competent judges of such important matters. Anyone who wants to approach God with the conviction of being heard must learn to restrain their heart from asking anything that is not according to His will. "You ask and do not receive, because you ask wrongly, to spend it on your passions" (James 4:3).

Instead of "good things," Luke 11:13 says the Holy Spirit. This does not exclude other benefits but points out what we really should ask for because we should never forget the encouragement: "Seek first the kingdom of God and his righteousness, and all these things will be added to you" (Matt. 6:33). When Christians pray, it is their duty to strip themselves of earthly desires and rise to meditation on the spiritual life. This is how they will put little value on food and clothing compared to the promise of their adoption (Rom. 8:15, Eph. 1:14:). If God has given such a valuable treasure, He will not refuse smaller favors.

Daily Reflection

Most of us will probably have heard the phrases, "Ask, seek, knock" before. It may be used in church or in other situations, but it has become a popular saying that is often misquoted. Calvin's very simple approach brings it back into context for us to understand. Jesus would never have said it if it was not going to happen that way. The problem comes when we use it for our own gain, or we misuse it. The key to this concept of asking and receiving is in the heart, whether we have God's will in mind or not.

1. Calvin says we can be convinced and confident when we approach God with our requests. Do you feel this way when you ask for things?
2. What does *"good things"* mean, according to Calvin?
3. How does this shift the meaning of what we ask, seek, and knock for?
4. What does Calvin mean when he says, *"strip themselves of earthly desires"*?

8

CHRIST, OUR MEDIATOR

For there is one God, and there is one mediator between God and men, the man Christ Jesus.
—1 Tim. 2:5

Some people are guilty of changing the meaning of Jesus' role: they claim that Christ is the Mediator of *redemption*, but that Christians are mediators of *intercession*. This makes it as if Jesus had only performed a temporary mediation and left an eternal mediation to us Christians! This false understanding comes from those who give Jesus only a small portion of the honor due to Him.

The meaning in the Bible is very different and it can only be understood simply by believers who disregard this false interpretation. When John says, "If anyone does sin, we have an advocate with the Father, Jesus Christ the righteous" (1 John 2:1), does he only mean that we *once* had an advocate?

Isn't he rather giving Jesus the role of *eternal* intercession? What does Paul mean when he declares that Jesus "is at the right hand of God, who indeed is interceding for us" (Rom. 8:34)? And then in the above verse he says that Jesus is the only Mediator between God and man. Isn't he referring to the supplications that he had mentioned a few verses before that (1 Tim. 2:1-2)? Having previously said that prayers should be said for all men, he immediately adds in confirmation of that statement that there is *"one God, and there is one mediator between God and men."*

Augustine's interpretation of this passage has the same meaning when he says,

Christians mutually encourage each other in their prayers. But He, for whom no one intercedes, while He Himself intercedes for all, is the only true Mediator. Though the Apostle Paul was a principal member under the Head, yet because he was a member of the body of Christ and knew that the most true and High Priest of the church had entered the inner sanctuary of heaven to holiness, he also followed the command to pray for the believers (Rom. 15:30; Eph. 6:19; Col. 4:3).

Paul does not make himself a mediator between God and the people but asks that everyone who is a member of the body of Christ should pray for each other, since they are communally sympathetic to each other: if one of them suffers, the others also suffer (1 Cor. 12:25-26).

So, the mutual prayers of all Christians rise up to Jesus the Head, who has gone before us into heaven and in whom there is forgiveness and appeasement for our sins (1 John

2:2). If Paul was a mediator, then the other Apostles would also be mediators. If that were true, then there would be many mediators, and Paul's statement would not make sense: *"There is one God, and there is one mediator between God and men, the man Christ Jesus;"* in whom we also are one (Rom. 12:5); if we keep "the unity of the Spirit in the bond of peace" (Eph. 4:3).

Carrying on from this idea, Augustine makes this comment on another passage in the Bible: "If you require a priest, He is above the heavens, where He intercedes for those on earth who He died for" (Heb. 7:26). We cannot think that Jesus actually falls down on His knees before His Father and intercedes for us. But we can understand, as Paul explains, that He appears in the presence of God and that the power of His death has the effect of an eternal intercession for us (Rom. 8:34). Having entered into the throne room, He alone continues to the end of the world to bring the prayers of His people, who are standing far off in the outer court, to God (Heb. 9:24).

Daily Reflection

The concept of Jesus as a mediator is very much in line with Him interceding for us. In the same way, an advocate stands in the gap between the judge and the accused, Jesus is the one who is our go-between. No one else can perform that role, not Mary, not the saints, or any other revered person. Our understanding of what Jesus has done and what He continues to do in maintaining our relationship with the Father is important to our prayer lives.

1. What is your understanding of a mediator?
2. What was the priest's role in the Old Testament? For more understanding, Hebrews 5, 6, and 7 are good to read.
3. Read Hebrews 9:15. How does this further the concept of Jesus as mediator?
4. Do you ever pray in "Jesus' name"? Why do you think it might be important?

9

A PRAYER OF FAITH

Answer me when I call, O God of my righteousness!
You have given me relief when I was in distress.
Be gracious to me and hear my prayer!
—Ps. 4:1

In this psalm, David's faith is shown. Although he was at the breaking point, with many things going wrong, he did not sink in sorrow, nor was he so broken in his heart to stop him from going to God, his deliverer. By praying, he testified that when there is no more earthly help or comfort, there is still hope in God. He calls Him the God of his righteousness, and he appeals to God, because everyone had condemned him, and all the rumors and judgments had smeared his innocent name. While there is nothing more painful than to be falsely accused and to have to endure wrongful violence and slander, to be spoken of badly for doing the right things is something most Christians have to go through. There is no other way but to turn away from all the enticements of the world and to depend completely on God alone.

In this verse, righteousness means a good cause, as David shows himself to God, while he complains of the malicious and wrongful behavior of people toward him. His example teaches us that if our uprightness is not seen and acknowledged by the world, we should not be discouraged because we have one in heaven who vindicates our cause. It is a comfort to know when people wrongfully push themselves over us that we are standing in the sight of God and of the angels. Paul was filled with courage in this way (1 Cor. 4:5) because when many evil stories were spread about him among the Corinthians, he appealed to the judgment seat of God. Isaiah was also strengthened by the same confidence (Isa. 50:6-7) when he did not consider all the rumors his enemies spoke against him. If we cannot find justice anywhere in the world, the only strength for us is to look to God and to rest content with his judgment.

Some people may object and say that everything good in people is just pollution in the sight of God, so how can the godly dare to bring forward their own righteousness before Him? When looking at David's prayer, it is easy to answer this question. He did not boast of his own righteousness except in reference to his enemies, from whose rumors and false allegations he justified himself. He had the testimony of a good conscience that he had attempted nothing without the call of God, and therefore, he does not speak out of turn when he calls God the protector and defender of his rights.

So, we learn that David honored God with this title of praise to set him apart from the whole world.

The intensity of his grief and the sincerity of his prayers are shown when he asks twice to be heard. In the last part of the verse, he also shows where he expected to get what he needed from the mercy of God. As often as we ask anything from God, it is good for us to begin with this, and to beg Him to relieve our miseries according to His free goodness.

"You have given me relief when I was in distress."

Some people think that David promises himself what he had not yet experienced, and in exercising hope, anticipates God's grace that he would only have later. Instead, he mentions the benefits that he previously received from God, and this is what strengthens him against what he would face next. Christians should be used to reminding themselves of those things that strengthen their faith. There are many other verses similar to this, where David recalls many experiences where he had learned that God is always present with his own people and will never disappoint their desires to bring energy to his faith against terrors and dangers. The expression he uses is metaphorical, and he does this to show that a way of escape was opened up to him even when he was surrounded on every side.

Daily Reflection

Faith plays a major role in prayer. Without it, we're simply mouthing words, reciting them to the air. Unfortunately, we are all guilty of doing this at certain times in our lives. We become numb or dead to things of the spirit; our hearts are not engaged. Instead of belief, we are filled with mistrust and doubt. These are not the foundations for a powerful and effective prayer. It's why we need to be encouraged and reminded, even in our lowest moments, to reach out and believe—even if it is only with a mustard seed of faith.

1. How often do you pray with faith? If you rate your prayers out of 10, with 10 being 100% filled with burning faith, how do yours stack up?
2. How do you think David managed to have such faith in such a hard time?
3. What does righteousness have to do with faith? Read James 5:16.
4. Read Mark 9:23 and 24. What do you understand by this?

10

COMING TO THE THRONE

Since then we have a great high priest who has passed through the heavens, Jesus, the Son of God, let us hold fast our confession. For we do not have a high priest who is unable to sympathize with our weaknesses. Let us then with confidence draw near to the throne of grace, that we may receive mercy and find grace to help in time of need.
—Heb. 4:14-16

The Jews were used to the Levitical priesthood, where one man was chosen to go into the sanctuary, and by his prayer, he might reconcile them all to God. Jesus, however, did not only succeed in glory but was also given kindness and compassion toward us.

"For we do not have a high priest who is unable to sympathize with our weaknesses."

We do not have to go far to find a Mediator, since Jesus extends His hand to us. We have no reason to fear the majesty of Jesus since He is our brother, and He took upon Him our weaknesses, that He might help us. This verse does not speak of what Jesus is in Himself but shows what He is to us. Jesus put on our flesh and also its feelings and emotions, so He not only lived as a real person but had also been taught by his own experience to help those who are weak and miserable. The Son of God did not need such training, but without it, we could not understand the care He feels for our salvation. So, whenever we are burdened by the weaknesses of our flesh, let us remember that the Son of God experienced the same, that He might raise us up by His power so that we are not overwhelmed by them.

He not only became a man, but he also assumed all the qualities of human nature—without sin. We must remember this difference between Jesus' feelings and ours, that His feelings were always regulated according to the strict rule of justice, while ours flow from a chaotic fountain and are wild and uncontrolled.

"Let us then with confidence draw near to the throne of grace."

Access to God is open to everyone who comes to Him relying on Jesus the Mediator. We are encouraged to come without any hesitation to present ourselves before God. And the main benefit is having bold confidence in calling on God. Christianity falls to the ground and is lost when this assurance is removed.

In some churches, the light of the Gospel is extinct, because people are taught to doubt whether God is favorable to them or is angry with them. They are told that God must be sought, but the way to come to Him is not pointed out, and the only gate through which people can enter is closed. They confess in words that Jesus is a Mediator, but they make the power of His priesthood ineffective and deprive Him of His honor. Jesus is not really known as a Mediator unless every doubt about our access to God is removed, otherwise, the conclusion would not be true: We have a High Priest who is willing to help us, therefore, we may come boldly and without any hesitation to the throne of grace. And if we are convinced that Jesus is stretching out His hand to us, who of us would not come in perfect confidence?

The assurance is that the throne of God is not only displayed in majesty, but it is decorated with grace, which we must remember whenever we would rather avoid the presence of God. When we only think of the glory of God, it can fill us with despair because His throne is so awesome. To overcome our hesitancy and free our minds from all fear, the throne is covered with *"grace,"* and gives it a name that appeals to us. Since God has displayed His throne with the banner of grace and His fatherly love toward us, there are no reasons why His majesty should drive us away. We can call on God without fear since we know that He is favorable to us, and this may be done because of the benefit given to us by Jesus (Eph. 3:12).

"That we may receive mercy."

This is not added for no reason—it is to encourage those who feel the need for mercy, so no one is left out because of their misery. This expression contains this wonderful truth that everyone who relies on the advocacy of Jesus, prays to God, and is sure of receiving mercy.

"To help in time of need."

This is added if we want to receive everything we need for our salvation. It refers to the time of calling according to Isaiah's words, "Behold, now is the favorable time" (Isa. 49:8; 2 Cor. 6:2) and Paul refers to "today," as the time when God speaks to us. If we only hear tomorrow, when God is speaking to us today, the night will come when it can no longer be done. We will knock in vain when the door is closed.

Daily Reflection

The throne of God might be a concept that is not easily or fully understood by modern Christians since kings are not what they were back in biblical times. Coming into a monarch's presence is foreign to most of us, let alone bowing before the throne. So, it is important to grasp this idea of God's throne and Jesus' role as a high priest if we want to appreciate how it relates to us coming with our prayers.

1. What is the throne of God?
2. Why is it important that Jesus had to suffer and experience weaknesses as a human?
3. How does this bring us confidence when we pray?
4. Why is important that this is a throne of grace and not judgment?

11

THE PHARISEE'S PRAYER

For everyone who exalts himself will be humbled, but the one who humbles himself will be exalted.
—Luke 18:14

Jesus talks about an attitude necessary for prayer. Christians must not come into the presence of God without humility. No disease is more dangerous than arrogance, and yet we all have it so deeply fixed in us, that it is difficult to remove. It is strange that people are crazy enough to elevate themselves and display their own merits before God. When we come into the presence of God, all pride should be put aside, but we think we have humbled ourselves enough if we just say a hypocritical prayer for forgiveness.

Jesus points out two offenses: wicked confidence in ourselves and the pride of despising others—one comes from the other.

It is impossible for a person who deceives themselves with arrogant confidence not to lift themselves up above others. Every person puffed up with self-confidence declares open war with God and cannot be reconciled in any other way than by denying themselves—laying aside all confidence in their own character and righteousness and relying on His mercy alone. The Pharisee, full of outward holiness, commends himself before God as if he had the right to offer a sacrifice of praise. He was rejected because he trusted in himself that he was righteous, and despised others.

"God, I thank you" (Luke 18:11). He is blamed for trusting that God was reconciled to him because of his own works. As he places reliance on works and prefers himself to others, both he and his prayer are rejected. People are not truly and properly humbled unless they doubt the merits of their works and learn to place their salvation in the goodness of God and put all their confidence in that.

This is an incredible parable because some think it is enough if they take away the glory of good works, which are gifts of the Holy Spirit, and admit that we are justified because God sees no righteousness in us except what He has given. But Jesus goes further by stripping us of all confidence in works. The Pharisee was not blamed for claiming for himself what belongs to God, but because he trusted his works, that God would be reconciled to him because he deserved it. Even though a person gives God the praise of works, if they imagine the righteousness of those works to be the cause of their salvation, they are condemned for wicked arrogance. Notice that the Pharisee is not charged with the selfish ambition of those who boast before others, while they are conscious of their own wickedness, but is charged with hidden hypocrisy. Though he did not proclaim the honor of his own righteousness aloud, his inner pride was offensive in the sight of God. His boasting has two parts: first, he clears himself of that guilt everyone else has; and, secondly, he boasts of his character. He claims he is not like others because he has not committed crimes that everyone else has.

"I fast twice a week; I give tithes of all that I get" (Luke 18:11). This is the same as saying he did more than the law required, just as the monks talk proudly of their works as if they found no great difficulty in fulfilling the law of God. But there are two things here that we must notice: we must not puff with confidence as if we have satisfied God, and we must not look down with contempt on others. In these, the Pharisee failed, because in falsely claiming righteousness for himself, he left nothing to the mercy of God, and he despised all others in comparison to himself. But as a proud hypocrite, by winking at his sins, he met the justice of God with a facade of complete and perfect righteousness; his wicked and detestable self-assurance made him fall. The only hope for Christians, so long as they are under the weakness of the flesh, is, after acknowledging what is good in them, to come to the mercy of God and rest their salvation on prayers for forgiveness.

But how did this man, who was blinded by wicked pride, maintain such holiness in life? This integrity only comes from the Spirit of God who does not live in hypocrites. He trusted his physical appearance as if the hidden uncleanness of the heart would not be taken into account. Even though he was full of wicked desires, he looked only at the outside and boldly maintained his innocence.

Daily Reflection

Luke 18 holds one of Jesus' most startling parables, where he compares two men coming into the temple to pray. The differences between them could not be more obvious, and it provides a clear picture for everyone of how God sees prayers. This first half deals with a Pharisee: a well-respected man of religion who was educated and trained in the ways of God. However, despite his outward appearance, he was arrogant and enjoyed his status.

1. Why is humility such a crucial aspect when it comes to prayer?
2. How often do you come to God in the same way or attitude as the Pharisee?
3. Why do you think this happens?
4. What does it mean that Jesus strips us of our "works"?

12

THE TAX COLLECTOR'S PRAYER

But the tax collector, standing far off, would not even lift up his eyes to heaven, but beat his breast, saying, "God, be merciful to me, a sinner!"
—Luke 18:13

The tax collector acts as if he had been some outcast, knowing that he is unworthy to approach, and presents himself with trembling and a humble confession.

Jesus did not intend to lay down a general rule whenever we pray, that we must turn our eyes down to the ground. He is just describing the signs of humility to his disciples. Humility is found in acknowledging our sins, condemning ourselves as we anticipate the judgment of God, looking to being reconciled to God, and making an honest confession of guilt. This is the reason for the feeling of shame that always comes with repentance. Jesus insists on this point, that the tax collector sincerely acknowledged himself to be miserable and lost and ran to the mercy of God. Even though he is a sinner, he trusts in forgiveness and hopes that God will be gracious to him. To gain favor, he admits that he does not deserve it. Since it is the forgiveness of sins that can only reconcile God to us, we must begin with this, if we want Him to accept our prayers. Anyone who acknowledges that they are guilty and convicted, and then continues to beg for forgiveness, denies any confidence in works. Jesus' aim here was to show that God will not be gracious to anyone except those who come trembling to His mercy.

"This man went down to his house justified, rather than the other" (Luke 18:4). The tax collector was accepted by God, while the Pharisee was totally rejected. And this verse shows us clearly the meaning of the word justified: it means to stand before God as if we were righteous. It does not say that the tax collector was justified because he suddenly gained some new quality, but that he found grace, because his guilt was wiped out, and his sins were washed away. So, we can see that righteousness consists in the forgiveness of sins. The virtues of the Pharisee were corrupted and polluted by unfounded confidence, so that his integrity, which deserved praise before the world, was of no value in the sight of God. But, the tax collector, not relying on the value of works, gained righteousness only by asking for forgiveness, because he had no other reason for hope than the pure mercy of God.

We may think it is ridiculous for everyone to be reduced to the same level since the purity of Christians is very different from that of the tax collector. But we must understand that whatever proficiency any of us have in worshiping God and

John Calvin on Prayer

in true holiness, if we see how far we really are, there is no other prayer we can say than starting with acknowledging our guilt. Because even though some are more, and others less, all of us are universally guilty. We cannot doubt that Jesus lays down a rule in this respect: God will not be pleased unless we denounce works and pray that we may be freely reconciled. Our faith needs no other support than this: that God has accepted us, not because we deserved it, but because He does not impute our sins.

Daily Reflection

The second part of this parable from Luke 18 is a complete contrast to the former half. Jesus cleverly chooses a tax collector as the other character for his story since they were rejected by many Jews as turncoats, double agents, or traitors. Unlike the Pharisees, they were already discarded as being worthy of God hearing them. In doing so, Jesus gives a short but sharp rebuke to all those listening then and reading now.

1. What made the tax collector's prayer so different?
2. Does humility mean beating ourselves down, feeling as bad as we can for who we are and what we've done?
3. Read John 3:30 and Romans 12:3. In your own words, what is humility?
4. Why does God accept us?

13

PRAYING IN CONFIDENCE

Before they call I will answer; while they are yet speaking I will hear.
—Isa. 65:24

It is strange that we are often not completely convinced of God's promises, or we become indifferent to them. Instead, we choose to wander up and down, neglecting the fountain of living waters, and would rather dig out broken reservoirs for ourselves (Jer. 2:13) than embrace the divine freedom offered to us.

"The name of the Lord is a strong tower; the righteous man runs into it and is safe" (Prov. 18:10). Joel, after predicting the terrible disaster that was coming, says the following unforgettable sentence: "And it shall come to pass that everyone who calls on the name of the Lord shall be saved" (Joel 2:32; Rom. 10:13). We know that this refers to the Gospel (Acts 2:21). Although only one out of a hundred might be moved to come into the presence of God, God still says, *"Before they call I will answer; while they are yet speaking I will hear."* He gives this same guarantee to the whole church, to all those in Christ: "When he calls to me, I will answer him; I will be with him in trouble; I will rescue him and honor him" (Ps. 91:15).

These are only a few verses to show how generously God draws us to Himself, and how ungrateful we are that even with such powerful encouragement, our laziness still holds us back. That is why these words should ring in our ears: "The Lord is near to all who call on him, to all who call on him in truth" (Psalm 145:18). Just like those verses from Isaiah and Joel, God also declares that His ear is open to our prayers and that He receives them like a sacrifice of sweet-smelling aroma when we cast our cares upon Him (1 Pet. 5:7; Ps. 55:22).

The special benefit of these promises we receive when we bring our prayer without doubt or hesitation, but trusting His Word, is that we can be bold and confident to call Him Father. He Himself suggests this wonderful name to us. Encouraged by such invitations, it is up to us to know that we have everything we need for prayer since our prayers do not depend on our own merit. All their worth and hope of success are based on and depend on the promises of God, so they need no other support.

We must be convinced that, even though we are not on the level of the early men of faith, prophets, and apostles, yet since the command to pray is for us as well as them, and we are in the same faith when we lean on the Word of God, we enjoy the same benefits as they did. When God declares in these verses that He will listen and be favorable to everyone, it encourages the least of us to have hope that we can still receive what we ask for.

All we need is a sincere heart, self-denial, humility, and faith so we don't blaspheme God's name when we pray. Our merciful Father will not reject those He encourages to come, because He also urges them in every possible way. So, this is why David can pray like this: "Therefore your servant has found courage to pray this prayer to you. And now, O Lord God, you are God, and your words are true, and you have promised this good thing to your servant" (2 Sam. 7:27-28). And in another passage, "Let your steadfast love comfort me according to your promise to your servant" (Ps. 119:76). And all the Israelites were encouraged by remembering the covenant that God spoke, and so they prayed with confidence (Gen. 32:13). In this way they copied the fathers of faith—especially Jacob—who, after confessing that he was not worthy of the blessing he had received from God, says that he is encouraged to still make big requests because God had promised that He would grant them (Gen. 32:10-13).

But when unbelievers run away from God, do not seek Him, nor ask for His help, they rob Him of His honor as if they were carving new gods and idols for themselves. This is how they deny that God is the author of all their blessings. But for Christians, nothing frees holy minds from doubts more than to be armed with the knowledge that no obstacle can stop them while they are obeying God's command because He said that nothing is better than obedience.

A confident spirit in prayer understands and knows fear, reverence, and anxiety. There is no inconsistency when God raises up those who have fallen down on their faces in prayer. In this way, phrases that appear inconsistent are actually in harmony with each other. Jeremiah and Daniel talk about humbly laying their supplications before God (Jer. 42:9; Dan 9:18). In another verse, Jeremiah says, "Let our plea for mercy come before you, and pray to the Lord your God for us, for all this remnant" (Jer. 42:2).

Christians are also told to lift up prayer. This is what Hezekiah means when he asks the prophet to pray (2 Kings 19:4). And David says, "Let my prayer be counted as incense before you, and the lifting up of my hands as the evening sacrifice!" (Ps. 141:2). The explanation is, that even though we as Christians know God's fatherly love for us, and we rely on His faithfulness with no hesitation to ask Him for help, we are not puffed with weak or arrogant security. Instead, as we climb up the ladder of the promises, we remain humble and petitioners.

Daily Reflection

These daily reflections do not have to be done in any specific order or time. You can come back to them, skip a question, or even spend all your time on only one aspect. They are not a series of exam queries to see if you pass or fail. They are here to trigger your thoughts, inspire you to see yourself in the context of the chapter, dig a little deeper into the Bible, and reflect on your own prayers. If you have more questions that come to mind, write them down and include them in your reflections.

1. How confident are you in your prayers? If you had to rate it out of 10, where would you score yourself?
2. Why do you think Christians are often not completely convinced of God's promises?
3. Why does Calvin lump confidence, fear, and anxiety into the same category?
4. What does "lift up prayer" mean?

14

A PRAYER OF REPENTANCE

I called out to the Lord, out of my distress, and he answered me.
—Jon. 2:1

When Jonah says that he prayed from the belly of the fish, he shows his attitude. He had put on a new heart because, before that, he thought he could escape from God and become a fugitive from the Lord. But now while he was imprisoned, he begins to pray, and of his own accord seeks God.

This change is worth noticing. We can learn how beneficial it is for us to be held back as though we were tied up because when we are free, we go astray all over the place. Jonah, when he was free, became lost. But now, finding himself restrained by the mighty hand of God, he receives a new mind and prays from the stomach of the fish.

Even while he is in this state of despair, Jonah found courage and was able to bring himself back to God. It is a wonderful and almost incredible example of faith. We learn that when the Lord afflicts us heavily, it is the best time for prayer. However, we know that most of us lose confidence and do not usually bring our prayers to God when we are anxious or down. And yet, this is when God invites us to Himself— when we are brought to the end of ourselves.

So, we can remember what Jonah says, that he cried to God from hell ("Sheol") itself; and at the same time, he tells us that his prayer came from true faith. He does not simply say that he prayed to Jehovah, but he adds that He was his God. Even though Jonah was almost like a dead person, confined to "hell," he still believed that God would be merciful if he ran to Him. From this, we see that Jonah did not pray randomly, as hypocrites do when they use God's name in times of trouble, but he prayed sincerely because he knew that God would be gracious to him. Christians do not gain victory without a great struggle. We must fight, sometimes violently so that we may conquer.

Jonah then shows that he was agitated with great trouble and tough challenges, yet this conviction was firmly fixed in his heart: that God was to be sought and would not be sought in vain. He is always ready to help His people whenever they cry to Him. Then Jonah says, *"I called out to the Lord, out of my distress, and he answered me."*

Once Jonah has related all his troubles, he then gives thanks to the Lord. This prayer contains two parts— that Jonah in his trouble fled to God—and the latter part contains thanksgiving for having been miraculously delivered beyond what flesh could have thought. "But I with the voice of thanksgiving will sacrifice to you; what I have vowed I will pay" (Jon. 2:9).

Jonah did not direct his prayers to God without a huge struggle; he faced many difficulties, but no matter how great they were, he still persevered and did not stop praying. He now tells us that he had not prayed in vain like those who pray to "idols.". To show the grace of God, he says that even in the depths of the grave when he was in distress, he was heard by the Lord.

When our flesh tells us that God is against us and that there is no more hope of forgiveness, faith sets up its shield and pushes back this attack of temptation. Faith brings back hope of forgiveness. Whenever God appears to be unforgiving, then our faith is tested. This was the state Jonah was in because according to the judgment of the flesh, he thought that he was completely thrown out by God so that he came to Him in vain. Jonah, still in his own power, could not immediately find the grace of God. Later though, he is full of thanksgiving. "Yet you brought up my life from the pit, O Lord my God" (Jon. 2:6).

After giving a long description to show that he did not physically die, but was overcome to the point of death, Jonah now adds his gratitude to the Lord for having delivered him.

He confirms what we see here in this chapter—that he did not pour out empty prayers, but that he prayed with sincerity, and he prayed in faith because he would not have called Him his God unless he was persuaded of his fatherly love, expecting to be saved. What follows immediately is that his prayer reached God. We can see that Jonah remembered his God, and through faith, knew that He would be gracious to him, and that was why he prayed.

Daily Reflection

The story of Jonah is a very well-known one, especially with kids. The storm and the big fish are always a highlight of this narration, and so often the critical point of his change of heart is overlooked for the more dramatic elements. He finally relents and turns to God as he somehow stays alive in the stomach of a large sea animal. In looking at his words, Calvin manages to extract some incredible gems for us to take for our own prayer lives. The deep emotion of Jonah's pleas to God becomes a challenge for our own times when we come before the Lord.

1. Do you think there is a place for emotion in prayer?
2. Why does Calvin highlight the importance of repentance in prayer?
3. Do you think repentance is a once-off affair when we're born again, or is it something we need to include more often in our prayers?
4. How does faith assist in us our times of doubt and grief?

15

REJOICE AND PRAY

Rejoice always, pray without ceasing, give thanks in all circumstances; for this is the will of God in Christ Jesus for you.
—1 Thess. 5:16-18

"*Rejoice always.*" This means having a consistent spirit when the mind is calm in hardships and does not give over to grief. In this, these three things are connected: to always rejoice, to pray without ceasing, and to give thanks to God in all things. When Paul recommends constant praying, he points to rejoicing continually, because this allows us to ask God for relief from all our distress. In the same way, Philippians 4:4-6 says, "Rejoice in the Lord always; again I will say, rejoice. Let your reasonableness be known to everyone. The Lord is at hand." And then Paul adds, "But in everything by prayer and supplication with thanksgiving let your requests be made known to God."

In these verses he shows the source of joy as a calm and composed mind that is not disturbed by injuries or hardships. In case we are weighed down by grief, sorrow, anxiety, and fear, he tells us to rest in the providence of God. And as doubts often appear as to whether God cares for us, he also gives the remedy—that by prayer we throw our anxieties into his arms, as David tells us to do in Psalm 37:5 and Psalm 55:22; and Peter in 1 Peter 5:7. But since we are so impulsive in our desires, he warns us to control them—that, while we desire what we are in need of, we do not cease to give thanks at the same time.

1 Thessalonians 5:16-18 almost has the same order as in Philippians but is said in fewer words. Paul wants us to admire God's goodness and blessings so much, that by recognizing them and meditating on them, we will overcome all sorrow. And if we consider what Jesus has given to us and done for us, there will be no bitterness or grief that cannot be alleviated and turned into spiritual joy. If this joy does not reign in us, the kingdom of God is banished from us, or we from it.

The person who is ungrateful to God is the one who does not value the righteousness of Jesus and the hope of eternal life. These are what make us rejoice in the midst of sorrow. Because our minds are so easily discouraged, becoming impatient, we must look at the remedy joined to the end of the verse. When we are down and laid low, we are lifted up again by prayers, because we lay on God what burdened us.

Every day and moment there are many things that can disturb our peace and ruin our joy, so, Paul tells us to pray without ceasing. Thanksgiving is added into this continual prayer as a limitation because many people, when they pray, murmur against God and worry if He does not immediately give them their wishes.

But, instead, it is good that our desires should be restrained this way so that, as we are content with what is given to us, we always mix thanksgiving with our desires. We can ask, sigh, and cry, but it must be in such a way that the will of God is more acceptable to us than our own.

For this is the will of God—that we give thanks. There is even more to it than this, though—that God is so biased towards us in Jesus, that even in our hardships, we have great opportunities for thanksgiving. What is better for calming us, than when we learn that God embraces us in Jesus so lovingly, that he turns everything that happens to us to our advantage and good? So, we can remember that this is a special cure for our impatience—to turn our eyes away from the current evil that troubles us and to look to something of a different nature—how God is moved toward us in Jesus.

Daily Reflection

Paul is one of the most respected writers of the New Testament because his letters make up the bulk of it. It's why, when he repeats certain things, we should sit up and take notice. The idea of rejoicing is one of those ideas that is found in more than one of his New Testament books.

1. What does it mean to "rejoice" and do you think it is possible to do this "always"?
2. Is this something that is a regular part of your prayers?
3. Why does Paul link rejoicing with prayer? Why does he add thanksgiving into it?
4. What is the will of God?

16

WHY WE PRAY

Continue steadfastly in prayer.
—Col. 4:2

There is an interaction between God and us, where we enter the throne room, and we come before Him and appeal to His promises. So, when we are in need, we can learn from experience that what we believed was not for nothing. In this, we see the Lord does not put anything before us that we are not told to ask of Him in prayer. Prayer digs up those treasures that the Gospel of Jesus reveals to us in faith. There are no words to describe how useful and beneficial prayer is to us.

Our heavenly Father says that our only safety is in calling upon His name (Joel 2:32). By His name, we call on His provision and take care of our needs, His power to sustain us when we are weak and almost fainting, and His goodness to receive us into favor, even though we are loaded with sin; we call upon Him to show Himself to us in all His glory. This is why peace comes to our minds because all our worries and needs are laid before the Lord. We can rest fully satisfied knowing that He knows everything, even our sins, and that He is both able and willing to provide the best for us.

Why We Must Pray

But someone will say, does He not already know our difficulties and what we need so that it might seem pointless to worry Him by our prayers, as if He was dozing or sleeping, and needs to be woken by the sound of our voice? Those who argue like this do not understand the reason Jesus taught us to pray.

It is not so much for *His* sake as it is for *ours*. He is honored when we acknowledge that everything we want, need, and pray to obtain, comes from Him. But even honoring Him is a benefit to us. That is why those in the Bible were confident when they proclaimed the mercies of God for themselves and others and were motivated to pray even more. We can look at the example of Elijah, who was so certain of God's promise of rain that he relayed it to Ahab, and yet he was still anxiously on his knees praying, sending his servant out seven times to check (1 Kings 18:42). He did not discredit the promise, but because he knew it was his duty to bring his desires before God so that his faith would not become lethargic or weak.

Even though we are sometimes lazy and apathetic, He wakes and watches for us and sometimes even helps us without us asking Him. It is for our own benefit that we constantly seek and ask Him:

- Our hearts will always be filled with a serious and sincere desire to seek, love, and serve Him, as we learn to see Him as our help and anchor in every circumstance.
- No selfish, foolish desires come into our minds, as we learn to bring all our wishes before Him as we pour out our hearts to Him.
- We are prepared to receive all His blessings with true gratitude and thanksgiving, while our prayers remind us that they come from His hand.
- When we have received what we asked for, knowing He has answered our prayers, we want more of His favor and are grateful for all the blessings that come through our prayers.
- Through experience, we understand His provision, knowing He does not only promise to never fail us, and spontaneously allows us to come to Him in times of need, but His hand is always stretched out to help us, not in empty words, but proving He is always supporting and helping us.

For these reasons, even though our Father in heaven never sleeps, He often seems to do so, to train us to not be lazy and indifferent when we ask, request, and beg Him to help us. It is illogical to discourage people from praying, by thinking

God's provision which watches over everything is not moved by our requests. Instead, the Lord Himself declares that He is "near to all who call on him, to all who call on him in truth" (Ps. 145:18).

It is also silly for people to think it is unnecessary to pray for things that the Lord has already decided to give us. It is for His pleasure that whatever comes from His spontaneous generosity should be acknowledged as being granted to our prayers. This is confirmed by the well-known verse in the Psalms: "The eyes of the Lord are toward the righteous and his ears toward their cry" (Ps. 34:15; 1 Pet. 3:12). This verse, while praising the care that God spontaneously gives all the believers, does not exclude having faith to wake our minds up from laziness. The eyes of God are open to help those who are blind to their needs, but He is also pleased to hear our groans so that He can prove His love to us even more.

So, we see that both parts of this verse are true: "He who keeps Israel will neither slumber nor sleep" (Ps. 121:4). And yet, whenever He sees us silent and lethargic, He withdraws as if He has forgotten us.

Daily Reflection

As Christians, we may have asked these questions at some point. Why bother if He already knows? Why ask if He has already decided? And yet, Calvin puts all those queries to rest in his simple, tactful, straightforward manner. Biblically, he shows what prayer is and why we engage in it. It is always good to be reminded of this as we sometimes lose sight and simply pray because it's expected of us.

1. In your own words, why do we pray?
2. Does it help or hinder you from praying, knowing God already knows?
3. What are the benefits of prayer for us as Christians?

17

PRAYING FOR FORGIVENESS

If we confess our sins, he is faithful and just to forgive us our sins and to cleanse us from all unrighteousness.
—1 John 1:9

Asking for forgiveness with a humble and sincere confession of guilt is the foundation and start for proper prayer. The holiest people cannot hope to get anything from God until they have been reconciled to Him. God cannot show favor to anyone except those whom He pardons. So, it is not strange that this is the key Christians use to open the door of prayer, as we see in the Psalms.

When David comes with another request, he says, "Remember not the sins of my youth or my transgressions; according to your steadfast love remember me, for the sake of your goodness, O Lord!" (Ps. 25:7). And later, "Consider my affliction and my trouble, and forgive all my sins" (Ps.

25:18). We can see that it is not enough to bring an account of the sins of each day, but we must also remember those that might seem to have been buried long ago in oblivion.

In another verse, when David is confessing a very serious crime, he goes all the way back to his birth, "Behold, I was brought forth in iniquity, and in sin did my mother conceive me" (Ps. 51:5). He does not do this to excuse the sin by highlighting how corrupt his nature is, but he does it to present the sins of his entire life. By being so strict in condemning himself, he hopes God might be more favorable to his request.

But, although we do not see a record of the early Christians always asking for forgiveness of sins, if we look carefully at their prayers in the Bible, the truth of what I am saying will become very clear. We can see that their courage to pray came purely from the mercy of God and that they always began their prayers by pleasing Him in this way. This is because, when Christians search their consciences, they do not presume to bring their concerns to God in an insincere manner. They know that if they did not trust in His mercy and forgiveness, they would be afraid to even come before Him.

Added to asking for forgiveness, there is another special confession. When Christians want to be delivered from punishment, they pray that their sins may be forgiven. It would be foolish to hope that the effect is taken away while the cause still remains. We must be careful of being like thoughtless hospital patients, who are so concerned with only curing the symptoms, that they neglect the root of the disease.

We have to first be reconciled with God before He will show His favor to us through physical acts. This is because it is the order He chooses. We cannot experience His kindness unless we know that He is first pleased with us—only then we are able to see Him as altogether lovely. We are reminded of this when we read Jesus' reply after he healed the paralyzed man. He said, "Take heart, my son; your sins are forgiven" (Matt. 9:2). In other words, He shows us what we should desire most of all: being right with God. He gives us the fruit of reconciliation by bringing assistance to us.

Besides the special confession of guilt that Christians use, when we ask for forgiveness for all our sins and punishment, that general introduction that brings favor to our prayers must never be left out. If we do, then our prayers will never reach God unless they come in through *free mercy*. Here, we must look at John's words: "If we confess our sins, he is faithful and just to forgive us our sins and to cleanse us from all unrighteousness" (1 John 1:9).

Under the Law, it was necessary to make prayers holy and pleasing through the atonement of blood (Gen. 12:8, 26:25, 33:20; 1 Sam. 7:9). In this way, they were made *acceptable*, and the people were also *warned* that they were unworthy of this privilege until being cleansed of sin, they then had confidence in prayer purely through the mercy of God.

Daily Reflection

Forgiveness is never easy. It's one of the reasons there are so many verses covering this topic in the Bible. Many Christians walk around with so much unforgiveness, yet they wonder why their prayers go unheard or unanswered. This can be a huge stumbling block in our prayer lives if we don't understand and apply it.

1. Why do you think Calvin sees asking for forgiveness as the start of prayer?
2. Why is confessing our sins so important? Who do we confess to?
3. What is the encouragement we receive in regard to confessing our sins?

18

THANKSGIVING IN PRAYER

I will give thanks to the Lord with my whole heart;
I will recount all of your wonderful deeds.
—Ps. 9:1

By prayer and supplication, we not only bring our desires before God, but we also ask for those things that promote His glory and display His name, since they are to our advantage. By thanksgiving, we celebrate His kindness to us, and how generously He gives us every blessing we receive. David used both of these in one sentence when he wrote, "Call upon me in the day of trouble; I will deliver you, and you shall glorify me" (Ps. 50:15). So, we can see that the Bible commands us to continually use both.

We have so many needs and hardships that there is enough reason for us to complain and groan to God without ever stopping, always begging. And even if we were free of troubles, even the holiest of us would still cry out to be saved because of their sins and temptations.

We would be guilty if we paused our sacrifice of praise and thanksgiving because God never stops giving us blessing upon blessing, so we are compelled to gratitude, however slow and lazy we are. So great are the riches of His generosity toward us, so marvelous and wonderful are the miracles we see, that there is no shortage of reasons for praise and thanksgiving.

To make this clearer: since all our hopes and resources are in God, so we cannot prosper without His blessing, we must constantly submit ourselves and everything we have to Him (James 4:14-15). Then whatever we think, speak, or do should be thought, spoken, and done through Him. And that is only because He assisted us.

God has cursed everyone who makes plans and decisions in their own strength and who try to carry these out without asking for His help (Isa. 30:1, 31:1). He receives the honor that is due to Him when we see Him as the Author of everything good. So, if we receive good things from Him, we should always express our gratitude. We also have no right to the benefits of His generosity if we do not praise Him and thank Him because that is why these gifts are given to us.

When Paul says that everything created by God "is made holy by the word of God and prayer" (1 Tim. 4:5), he means that without the word and prayers, none of them are holy and pure (*word* meaning *faith*). That is why David, when he experienced God's love, declares, "He put a new song in my mouth" (Ps. 40:3). So, our silence is wicked if we do not acknowledge His blessings because every blessing He gives us is a new reason for thanksgiving.

- Isaiah proclaims the mercies of God by saying, "Sing to the Lord a new song" (Isa. 42:10).
- David says, "O Lord, open my lips, and my mouth will declare your praise" (Ps. 51:15). Hezekiah, after he was delivered, says he will celebrate the goodness of God in the "house of the Lord" (Isa. 38:20)
- Jonah says, "With the voice of thanksgiving will sacrifice to you" (Jon. 2:10).

David gives Christians a general rule: "What shall I render to the Lord for all his benefits to me? I will lift up the cup of salvation and call on the name of the Lord" (Ps. 116:12-13). This rule for the church is also found here: "Save us, O Lord our God, and gather us from among the nations, that we may give thanks to your holy name and glory in your praise" (Ps. 106:47). And here:

He regards the prayer of the destitute and does not despise their prayer. Let this be recorded for a generation to come, so that a people yet to be created may praise the Lord... that they may declare in Zion the name of the Lord, and in Jerusalem his praise. (Ps. 102:17-18, 21)

Whenever we ask the Lord to do anything for His own name's sake, we say we are unworthy to receive it in our own name, so we give thanks and promise to proclaim His love. Hosea, when he speaks about the future redemption of the church, says, "Take with you words and return to the Lord; say to him, 'Take away all iniquity; accept what is good, and we will pay with bulls the vows of our lips'" (Hosea 14:2).

We do not just praise Him with our mouths, but our words are filled with love for Him. "I love the Lord, because he has heard my voice and my pleas for mercy" (Ps. 116:1).

Praise without this love does not please God. This is why Paul says all our requests are wicked if they do not come with thanksgiving. "In everything by prayer and supplication with thanksgiving let your requests be made known to God" (Phil. 4:6).

Many people who are depressed, tired, impatient, bitter, afraid, and sad, complain in their prayers. This is why Paul encourages us to control our feelings and be grateful and cheerful, so we can bless God before we are able to receive what we ask for. But if this connection ought always to subsist in full vigor between things that are almost contrary, the more sacred is the tie that binds us to celebrate the praises of God whenever He grants our requests.

Our prayers would be useless and wicked if they were not sanctified by the intercession of Jesus, which is why we are told to "continually offer up a sacrifice of praise to God" (Heb. 13:15). We are reminded that without the intervention of Jesus' priesthood, our lips are not pure enough to celebrate the name of God. Paul continues by saying, "Pray without ceasing, give thanks in all circumstances" (1 Thess. 5:17-18). He wants us to know that at all times, in every place, in all things, and under all circumstances, we must direct our prayers to God, to expect all the things that we desire from Him, and when obtained, praise Him for them.

Daily Reflection

Having your Bible close by is very helpful when learning anything about God. It helps to check, make sure, and dig deeper. It's great if you have a physical one with pages in your hands, as this stimulates your brain and memory more than a digital one, but it's not imperative. Looking up each scripture helps your mind to absorb what Calvin is saying, so it is not just his words, but the Bible speaking to you.

1. Many of the psalms are filled with thanksgiving. Read any of these for inspiration: Psalm 34, 86, 89, 92, 95, or 100.
2. Paul says our prayers are "wicked" if they don't come with thanksgiving. Do you agree?
3. What percentage of your prayers contains thanksgiving?

19

ALL OUR CARES TO HIM

Rejoice in the Lord always; again, I will say, rejoice. Let your reasonableness be known to everyone. The Lord is at hand; do not be anxious about anything, but in everything, by prayer and supplication with thanksgiving let your requests be made known to God. And the peace of God, which surpasses all understanding, will guard your hearts and your minds in Christ Jesus.
—Phil. 4:4-7

"**R**ejoice in the Lord."

This is always a good encouragement since dangers threaten us on every side, and it is possible we might fall or be overcome by grief or impatience. So, Paul says that, despite the hostility and trouble, we should still rejoice in the Lord, because the way the Lord refreshes us works best when the world tempts us to despair. In imprisonment, in the heat of persecution, and the apprehensions of death, Paul is not just joyful but even motivates us to joy. Whatever happens, Christians with the Lord standing on their side have enough reason for joy.

The repetition gives it even more emphasis: Let this be your strength and stability, to rejoice in the Lord, and that your joy in Him may be extended. This differs from the joy of the world—we know from experience that the joy of the world is deceptive, frail, and fading, and Jesus even says it is doomed (Luke 6:25). Only an established joy in God is one that can never be taken away from us.

"Let your reasonableness be known to everyone,"

Reasonableness, or in some translations, "moderation," is a Greek term to mean moderation of spirit—when we are not easily moved by pain when we are not easily annoyed by hardship but retain composure. Cicero used the following expression: "My mind is tranquil, which takes everything in good part."

"The Lord is at hand."

The more the wicked see us prepared to endure suffering, the more they want to hurt us, and it becomes difficult to keep our souls patient (Luke 21:19). We think that violence must be met with violence so that they may not insult us whenever they want. But Paul replies, saying the Lord is at hand, whose power can overcome their audacity, and whose goodness can conquer their hate. He promises that He will aid us, provided we obey His commandment. Now, wouldn't you rather be protected by the hand of God, than have all the resources of the world at your command?

From this idea, we learn that ignorance of God's provision is what causes all the impatience and that this is the reason why we are so quickly thrown into confusion, and we become discouraged because we do not recognize the fact that the Lord cares for us. On the other hand, we learn that this is the only cure to bring peace to our minds. We can rest in His care, knowing that we are not exposed to reckless fate or to the impulse of the wicked, but are under the order of God's fatherly care. Those who have this truth—that God is present with them—have what they need to rest with security.

"But in everything."

Paul encourages the Philippians, as David does in Psalm 55:22, and Peter in 1 Peter 5:7, to cast all their cares on the Lord. We are not made of iron and are shaken by temptations, but this is our support—to deposit or cast everything that harasses us onto God. Confidence brings peace to our minds, but this is only when we are praying. Whenever we are attacked by any temptation, let us run to prayer like a refuge.

The word *"requests"* means desires or wishes, and Paul wants us to make these known to God by prayer and supplication, as Christians pouring their hearts before God, when they commit themselves, and all that they have, to Him. Those who look around for the useless comforts of the world might appear to be relieved, but there is one sure refuge—leaning on the Lord.

"With thanksgiving."

Because many of us often pray to God incorrectly, full of complaints, as though we have good reason to accuse Him, while some of us cannot wait if He does not immediately give us our desires, Paul links thanksgiving with prayers. It is as though he said that those things which are necessary for us should be desired by us from the Lord in such a way that we surrender to His good pleasure and give thanks while presenting petitions. Gratitude will have this effect on us—that the will of God will be what we desire.

"And the peace of God, which surpasses all understanding, will guard your hearts and your minds in Christ Jesus."

This is a promise showing the advantage of firm confidence in God and appealing to Him. "If you do that," Paul says, "the peace of God will keep your minds and hearts." The Bible often separates the soul into two parts: the mind and the heart. The mind is the understanding, while the heart is the attitude or feelings. These two terms include the entire soul which makes the verse mean: "The peace of God will guard you, to prevent you from turning back from God in wicked thoughts or desires."

The peace of God does not depend on present circumstances and does not bend to the various events of the world, but is established on the solid, unchangeable word of God. Paul speaks of it as surpassing all understanding because nothing is stranger to the human mind than in the depth of despair to have a feeling of hope, in the depth of poverty to see riches, and in the depth of weakness to keep from falling, and to promise ourselves that nothing will be deficient when we are left destitute of all things. All of this only happens in the grace of God, which is known through the word, and the inner sincerity of the Spirit.

Daily Reflection

As humans, we are prone to worry. It is in our nature to be concerned and anxious about things that are out of our control—some of us more than others. It is why the Bible continually reminds us to not worry. This seems hard, but one of the benefits of prayer is being able to hand it all over to God.

1. Do you worry a lot? What about?
2. Do you find most of your prayer contains a list of issues you bring to God?
3. Is there a difference between telling God about something and laying it down before God?
4. Have you ever experienced the peace that passes understanding?

20

PRAYING CONTINUOUSLY

Praying at all times in the Spirit, with all prayer and supplication.
—Eph. 6:18

I agree when people say that circumstances that cause us to pray are not always equal.

This distinction is shown in James: "Is anyone among you suffering? Let him pray. Is anyone cheerful? Let him sing praise" (James 5:13). Therefore, common sense says that because we are too lazy, we must be stimulated by God to pray sincerely whenever the occasion requires. David calls this a time when God "may be found"—a seasonable time (Psalm 32:6; 31:6) because, as he declares in several other passages, the more intense the grievances, annoyances, fears, and other kinds of trials are that we experience, the freer our access is to God—as if He were inviting us to Himself.

And yet Paul's command to pray "at all times" (Eph. 6:18; 1 Thess. 5:17) is just as true because, even if everything is going well for us and we are filled with joy, there is no moment that our needs do not bring us to prayer. A person can have plenty of food and drink, but since he cannot enjoy a crumb of bread, except from the continuous generosity of God, his pantry will not prevent him from asking for daily bread. Then, if we consider how many dangers threaten us all the time, fear teaches us that no moment should be without prayer.

We can understand this better when it comes to spiritual matters. How can we sit back self-assured, knowing we will have no freedom from the guilt and punishment of our many sins unless we pray for it? When will temptation give us a break, making it unnecessary to ask for help? Passion for the kingdom and glory of God should not be sporadic, but continuous, so that every moment should be in season. So, there is a reason that diligence in prayer is encouraged so often.

When the Bible reminds us of the necessity of constant prayer (1 Thess. 5:17), it also accuses us of being lazy because we do not always feel the need to give it so much attention and diligence. This biblical rule also means hypocrisy and lying to God should be restricted, or even totally *banished* from prayer. God promises that He will be near to those who call on Him in truth (Ps. 145:18) and declares that those who seek Him with their whole heart will find Him (Jer. 29:13-14).

Everyone who is happy with their sin and polluted hearts cannot seek Him. One of the conditions of proper prayer is repentance. So, the common declaration of the Bible is that God does not listen to the wicked (John 9:31) and that their prayers (Prov. 28:9; Isa. 1:15) and their sacrifices (Prov. 15:8, 21:27) are an abomination to Him. Those who close their hearts will find the ears of God closed to them, and those who are hard in their hearts provoke Him to anger and will find Him 'stubborn and unyielding.'

In Isaiah, God threatens: "Even though you make many prayers, I will not listen; your hands are full of blood" (Isa. 1:15). And in the same way, in Jeremiah, "Though they cry to me, I will not listen to them" (Jer. 11:7-8, 11) because He sees it as the highest insult for the wicked to boast of His covenant while blaspheming His holy name by their whole lives. That is why He complains in Isaiah, "This people draw near with their mouth and honor me with their lips, while their hearts are far from me" (Isa. 29:13). This is not just confined to prayers, but He says He hates all hypocrisy in every part of His service.

This is why we see the words of James: "You ask and do not receive, because you ask wrongly, to spend it on your passions" (James 4:3). It is true that the righteous do not trust in themselves or their worth when they speak their prayers. So, the warning of John is not for nothing: "Whatever we ask we receive from him, because we keep his commandments and do what pleases him" (1 John 3:22).

An evil conscience shuts the door against us. Only sincere worshipers of God pray correctly or are listened to. Therefore, everyone who wants to pray must not be satisfied or content with anything that is wrong in their hearts. They cannot pray without repentance, which is the character and attitude of a petitioner.

Daily Reflection

Praying continuously seems like a very difficult task to achieve. For many of us, 10-30 minutes is about as much as we can physically handle. And yet, in the Bible, Paul's words are very clear in that prayer should not stop but be an ongoing exercise.

This issue is often a stumbling block for people who think they need to be mumbling sentences throughout the day with no pause. It's also a heavily debated subject, ending in rules and opinions on how, when, and where. How is it possible to pray continuously without ceasing? Is it literal or metaphorical? Here, Calvin doesn't get too involved in arguing the issue, but he simply points toward the attitude, not the act.

1. Have you ever prayed for an extended period? What helped you to keep going?
2. What makes it difficult for you to continue praying sometimes?
3. Do you agree with Calvin's view of what it means to pray continuously?
4. Read 1 Thessalonians 5:16-18. Why do you think Paul included so many commands in the same sentence?

21

PERSISTENCE IN PRAYER

They ought always to pray and not lose heart... And will not God give justice to his elect, who cry to him day and night?...when the Son of Man comes, will he find faith on earth?
—Luke 18:1, 7-8

We know that perseverance in prayer is difficult to achieve. Our unbelief is exposed when our first prayers are not successful, and we immediately throw away hope and all the devotion of prayer. But our faith is revealed when we are disappointed in our wish, and yet do not lose courage. So, Jesus recommends His disciples should persevere in praying.

The parable highlights how to be persistent in our prayers to God the Father until we finally get what we thought He was unwilling to give. Our prayers do not give us victory over God and bend Him to compassion, but He graciously listens to our prayers even when everything seems to point the other way. If the wicked and cold-hearted judge could not avoid giving in to the pleas of the widow, how can the persistent prayers of believers have no effect? If we get exhausted after much effort or if the passion of prayer fades because God appears to not hear, we must be reminded of our ultimate success, even though it does not look that way. With this conviction, let us not become impatient and stop our prayers because we have to wait.

"And will not God give justice to his elect, who cry to him day and night?"

Jesus does not compare God to a wicked and cruel judge but points out a very different reason why those who believe in Him are kept waiting, and why He does not immediately stretch out His hand to them. It is done with a fatherly intention: to train us to be patient. Temporarily overlooking crimes is very different from allowing them to go unpunished. The promise of giving us justice is according to His wisdom because our quick tempers and emotions make us think He does not come quickly enough to bring relief. But if we look into His design, we will learn that his assistance is always ready, timely, and is never late, but comes at the exact time.

God avenges us, not to give us free rein of our emotions but to convince us that our salvation is precious to Him, and we need to rely on His protection. If we are pure and free from every evil desire of revenge and hatred, and we ask for His assistance, it will be a righteous and holy wish, and God will listen to it. This is not always easy, and if we want to give pure, sincere prayers, we must ask the Lord to guide and direct our hearts by his Spirit.

"When the Son of man comes..."

Jesus teaches us that there is no reason to wonder if people will drown in their evil actions or not: it will happen because they do not accept the true remedy. Betrayal, cruelty, deceit, and violence are all around us; there is no concern for justice and no shame. The poor cry out under their oppressors; the innocent are abused or insulted, while God appears to be asleep in heaven. But Jesus reminds us that people have no heavenly help because they do not know about it or do not rely on it. Those who only murmur against the Lord in their hearts, and who allow no place for his provision, cannot expect the Lord to assist them.

"Will he find faith on earth?"

Jesus tells us clearly that until He returns, there will be many unbelievers. If He does not come back soon, it is because there are almost no people looking for Him. But, even though the world is oppressed and overwhelmed by evil and disasters, there are a few in whom the smallest spark of faith can be seen.

Daily Reflection

As modern Christians, persistence in prayer does not seem to be a strong point. Believers of old spent hours, even days before the Lord in prayer. We sometimes struggle to reach 15 minutes. There are lots of distractions and excuses. If we're honest, we lack discipline and passion. It is one of the reasons Jesus told this parable, to highlight this lack of determination and perseverance.

1. How long do you usually pray for? Do you feel it is enough?
2. Are you able to pray for something over an extended period of time? Weeks, months, maybe years?
3. Have you ever received an answer for something you have prayed for for a long time?
4. What do you think helps to increase persistence in prayer?

22

A PRAYER OF HELP

I wept and humbled my soul with fasting....
When I made sackcloth my clothing...
I am the talk of those who sit in the gate....
But as for me, my prayer is to you, O Lord.
At an acceptable time, O God, in the abundance
of your steadfast love answer me in your saving faithfulness.
—Ps. 69:10-13

"I wept and humbled my soul with fasting."

David proves that his efforts to promote God's glory came from a pure passion: not from physical emotions, but from humbly surrendering himself before God. He reveals the wickedness of his enemies, showing he was oppressed with such violence by his enemies that he dared not open his mouth to defend God and had nothing else but tears and mourning. He says he *"made sackcloth [his] clothing,"* which showed mourning among the Jews, but his enemies mocked him for this. It is an important example for us, not to be discouraged when we experience the same things. Instead, we must beware of pouring oil on the fire, which is already burning too fiercely, and should rather imitate David and Lot who were deeply grieved in their hearts.

"I am the talk of those who sit in the gate."

David complains that he became a *"byword"* by the elite. Although people of every status and condition were at the gates, only the judges and counselors sat there. It was a very cruel treatment that this holy man was not only harassed by the lower classes but by those meant to bring justice and the dignitaries of the church. As the same thing happens today, the Holy Spirit shows this as an example to us. The higher a leader is exalted in honor (even in the church), he is as violent and outrageous in his opposition to the Gospel and its ministers. Almost all rulers fall into this trap because they think they are entitled to act as they please. They mock and ridicule Christians to shame them into renouncing their faith, laughing at their simplicity as if they are fools wasting their time serving God.

"But as for me, my prayer is to you, O LORD."

It was a sign of rare character in David, that even this hard treatment could not shake his mind and sink him into discouragement. He tells us how he strengthened himself against that terrible stumbling block. When the wicked made their clever, mocking remarks to undermine his faith, the method he used to repel their attacks was to pour out his heart in prayer to God. He kept silent before men and brought himself to God. In the same way, although Christians today might not be able to make any impression on the wicked, they will ultimately find victory if they draw back from the world and go directly to God with their prayers.

David had tried everything in his power, and when he saw his efforts were useless, did not deal with men, but only with God. What followed was meeting with God at *"an acceptable time"* which links to Isaiah 55:6, "Call upon him while he is near." Other translations explain it as 'I prayed that the time of favor might come and that God would begin to be merciful to me.' But David is speaking of the comfort he received by reflecting with himself, that although it was a time of trouble for him, and although his prayers seemed to be unsuccessful, God's favor would also have its turn.

In the same way, Habakkuk says, "I will take my stand at my watchpost and station myself on the tower, and look out to see what he will say to me" (Hab. 2:1).

And Isaiah makes a similar statement: "I will wait for the LORD, who is hiding his face from the house of Jacob, and I will hope in him" (Isa. 8:17).

Jeremiah also says, "So we will wait for you to help us" (Jer. 14:22 NLT).

The only way we can have victory in our suffering is by hope shining in us in the midst of darkness, and by the sustenance that comes from waiting for the favor of God. After David was strengthened to continue waiting, he immediately added, "Answer me, O Lord, for your steadfast love is good." He joins God's goodness with the truth of salvation, showing that God's mercy is real when He comforts His servants who are in the depths of despair. What made David say this prayer was that he believed that the darkness he was in at the time would soon be over and that a calm and unclouded season of God's favor would follow. It was a belief that came because he shifted all his thoughts onto God so that he would not fall because of the cruel treatment of the wicked.

Daily Reflection

The psalms are more than just songs of gratitude and poems of victory, they are also honest cries to God. Here, David bares his soul as he comes before the Lord. One of the keys is that he comes only to God for deliverance, not to anyone else. This is what makes his prayer so rich and real. He cries out to God.

1. Do you ever "cry" out to God in prayer?
2. How often do you turn to God in prayer after trying other plans and avenues for help?
3. What does Calvin say is the only way we can have victory in suffering?

23

WATCH AND PRAY

And going a little farther, he fell on his face and prayed, "My father, if it be possible, let this cup pass from me; nevertheless, not as I will, but as you will." And he came to the disciples and found them sleeping. And he said to Peter, "Watch and pray that you may not enter into temptation. The spirit indeed is willing, but the flesh is weak."
—Matt. 26:41

"And going a little farther."

In other passages, to experience deeper prayer, the Lord prayed without anyone around Him. When we are out of sight of others, we can gather our senses better and focus on what we are doing. It is not necessary to go off to distant corners whenever we pray, but there are times when the passion of prayer is more freely experienced when we are alone, then it is good for us to pray alone. And if the Son of God did this, it would simply be pride for us not to do the same for our own advantage. Also, when God is the only witness, and there is no ambition, the believing soul opens with more familiarity and with more simplicity pours its wishes, groans, anxieties, fears, hopes, and joys, to God. God allows His people to use many ways of speaking when they pray alone, which would not be acceptable in other people's presence.

"He fell on his face."

In the act of falling on the earth, Jesus showed His deep sincerity in prayer. Even though kneeling—our expression of respect and reverence—is commonly used in prayer, Jesus showed His grief by throwing Himself on the ground as a petitioner.

"My Father, if it be possible."

Some people claim this is not a prayer, only a complaint. But there is no doubt that Jesus offered a prayer. The prayers of Christians do not always flow with unbroken progress to the end, do not always keep a steady measure, and are not always arranged in a distinct order. They are involved and confused, and either conflict or stop in mid-sentence, like a ship tossed by waves, that cannot always keep a straight course even though it's headed for the harbor. Jesus did not have confused emotions, like those we often have. He was struck with fear and seized with anguish, so that, in the violent shocks of temptation, He jumped from one wish to another. This is why, after having prayed to be freed from death, He immediately restrains Himself and, submitting to the authority of the Father, corrects and retracts that wish.

"Not as I will, but as you will."

We see how Jesus controls His feelings, quickly bringing Himself into a state of obedience. In us all, the emotions of the flesh break out into rebellion or are not completely holy, but Jesus, in the grip of grief or fear, restrained Himself. Just as two musical sounds, though different, are so far from being discordant that they produce sweet melody and fine harmony, so in Jesus, there is the example of adaptation between the two wills—the will of God and the will of man—so that they differed from each other without any conflict or opposition.

"And he came to the disciples."

Even though He was not delivered from fear or anxiety, He stopped His prayer. We are supposed to be constant in prayer with God, but just as Jesus did, we continue our prayers until we have gone as far as our strength allows, then stop for a short time, and immediately after catching our breath, return to God. Even though He did not need anyone's assistance, the indifference of His disciples added a heavy and distressing burden to his grief. He declares He is grieved at having been forsaken and had good reason for rebuking them because they did not watch even one hour.

"Watch and pray."

Jesus threatens that, if they do not watch and pray, they may be soon overwhelmed by temptation. To enter into temptation means to yield to it. The manner of resistance we are to have is not to find courage in our own strength and perseverance, but from a conviction of our weakness, to ask for strength from the Lord. Our watching will be useless without prayer.

"The spirit indeed is willing."

Instead of alarming his disciples, he gently rebukes their laziness and adds consolation of hope. He reminds them that even though they want to do what is right, they still have to contend with the weakness of the flesh, so prayer is always necessary. He praises their willingness so that their weakness may discourage them, but still urges them to pray because they are not properly filled with the power of the Spirit. We also want to do what is right, but still strive under the weakness of the flesh, because even though the grace of the Spirit is in us, we are weak according to the flesh. Just as Jesus warns His disciples, it is our duty to diligently keep watch by praying, because we do not yet have enough of the power of the Spirit to keep us from the weakness of the flesh, unless the Lord gives His assistance to raise up and uphold us. We do not need to worry, as Jesus promises that everyone who is sincere in prayer will perseveringly oppose the laziness of the flesh and will be victorious.

Daily Reflection

Again, we see the issue of perseverance in prayer, but this time from Jesus. The scene is in the garden where He was betrayed. After a long night, the disciples were tired and struggled to stay awake. They did not understand the urgency of the moment. Jesus rebuked them more than once, asking why they could not stay awake and pray. We often have the same problem, running out of energy and unable to push into the presence of God.

1. How would you rate your perseverance in prayer?
2. If there is a prayer meeting at church, do you do everything you can to be there or is it too much effort?
3. What is the benefit of persevering in prayer?

24

MARY'S PRAYER

My soul magnifies the Lord, and my spirit rejoices in God my Savior. For he has looked on the humble estate of his servant. For behold, from now on all generations will call me blessed; for he who is mighty has done great things for me, and holy is his name. And his mercy is for those who fear him from generation to generation.
—Luke 1:46-50

The song of Mary starts with thanksgiving for the mercy of God she had experienced.

"My soul magnifies the Lord."

Here Mary shows her gratitude. While hypocrites mostly sing the praises of God from their mouths without any feeling in the heart, Mary praises God from an inner feeling of the mind. Those who only pronounce His glory with the tongue and not the mind only disrespect His holy name. The words 'soul' and 'spirit' are used in the Bible in different senses, but, when used together, they speak about the spirit in terms of understanding, and the soul as the emotions.

The motivation to praise God must first come from rejoicing in the spirit, as James says, "Is anyone cheerful? Let him sing praise" (James 5:13.) Sadness and anxiety lock up the soul and restrict the tongue from celebrating God's goodness. When Mary's soul bursts with joy, the heart breaks out in praising God.

In speaking of the joy of her heart, she calls God her Savior. Until God is recognized as a Savior, the minds of people are not free to experience true and full joy but will remain in doubt and anxiety. It is only by God's fatherly kindness, and the salvation that comes from it, that the soul is filled with joy. So, the first thing for Christians is to be able to rejoice that they have their salvation in God. Then, having experienced God to be a kind Father, they can "offer to God a sacrifice of thanksgiving" (Ps. 50:14). The Greek word for Savior has more meaning than in Latin because it not only means that He delivers once, but that He "became the source of eternal salvation" (Heb. 5:9).

"For he has looked."

She explains the reason why her joy is from God, that in grace He had looked upon her. By calling herself humble, she denies any honor and finds every chance to boast about the undeserved goodness of God. Humility does not mean being ignorant and uneducated. Instead, it says, "I was unknown and despised, but that did not prevent God from seeing me" (1 Thess. 5:20). This was not the loud cry of a pretended humility, but the plain and honest statement of a conviction engraved on her mind because she was nothing in the eyes of the world, and she saw herself as nothing more.

"All generations will call me blessed."

She says that God's kindness will be remembered throughout all generations and that her honor comes only from what God has given to her as the gift of His grace. She did not say this for her own glory or honor, since she only speaks about the work of God. This is completely opposite to those religious hypocrites who exalt her by calling her "Queen of Heaven, Star of Salvation, Gate of Life, Sweetness, Hope, and Salvation." In doing so, they give her authority over Jesus.

None of these names were given to her by Jesus. All of them are refuted by Mary when she says that her only glory is in God's kindness. If her duty was to only praise the name of God, who had done wonderful things for her, there is no room for made-up titles. Nothing could be more disrespectful to her than to rob the Son of God of what belongs to Him.

"He who is mighty has done great things for me."

The second and third parts of Mary's song celebrate God's power and judgments, and then look at the salvation promised and given to the church.

"And holy is his name."

Here, Mary celebrates the power, judgments, and mercy of God. This part must not be read separately from the first part. Mary had praised the grace of God, which she had personally experienced. That is why she takes the opportunity to say, *"Holy is His name,"* and *"His mercy is for those who fear him from generation to generation."* The name of God is called holy because it deserves the ultimate reverence, and whenever the name of God is mentioned, it should immediately remind us of His wonderful majesty.

The next clause, which celebrates God's endless mercy, is taken from the covenant: "I will establish my covenant between me and you and your offspring after you throughout their generations for an everlasting covenant" (Gen. 17:7). And also when it says, "…who keeps covenant and steadfast love with those who love him and keep his commandments, to a thousand generations" (Deut. 7:9).

By these words, God not only declares that He will always be Himself but expresses the favor He continues to show His own people, even after their death, loving their children, and their children's children. "But the steadfast love of the Lord is from everlasting to everlasting on those who fear him, and his righteousness to children's children, to those who keep his covenant and remember to do his commandments" (Ps. 103:17-18).

Daily Reflection

As we have already read, there is only one to whom and through whom we should pray. Praying to anyone else like Mary or saints does not line up with the Bible. However, as Jesus' mother, her obedience is still a remarkable example to be noted. This record of her song/prayer is often overlooked, but it holds some incredible truths to learn about prayer.

1. What do you think of the opening line? Do your prayers ever begin in similar fashion?
2. This is a celebration of God and all His attributes. Have you ever devoted a prayer completely to praising and worshiping God for who He is and what He has done?

25

HOW TO PRAY

Now Jesus was praying in a certain place, and when he finished, one of his disciples said to him, "Lord, teach us to pray.
—Luke 11:1

Firstly, everyone who prays should focus all their thoughts and feelings and not be distracted by wandering thoughts (as often happens). For nothing is more contrary to the reverence God deserves than the carelessness of our minds when given too much freedom or when there is no godly fear. So, we should make more effort if this is something we struggle with because anyone who wants to pray will experience many thoughts creeping in, either changing the direction of the prayer or disrupting it in some way.

Think how inappropriate it is when God turns to listen to us and then we abuse His attention by mixing holy things with irreverent things. We are disrespectful when we don't control our minds, but instead, in our prayers, act as if we were chatting with some ordinary person, forgetting God, by letting our thoughts run wild. The only people who are prepared for prayer are those who are so in awe of God's majesty that they pray without thinking of everyday concerns or their feelings.

The act of lifting up our hands in prayer is designed to remind us that we are far from God unless our thoughts rise upward. As it says in the Bible, "To you, O Lord, I lift up my soul" (Ps. 25:1). The Bible often uses the expression to "lift up our prayer" (Isa. 37:4), meaning that those who want to be heard by God must not "settle on [their] dregs" (Jer. 48:11). That God freely invites us to bring our burdens to Him leaves us with no excuse but to be in awe of Him, since He is more important than everything else. In response, our prayer should seriously occupy every thought and feeling. This cannot happen unless our mind, fighting against every weakness and temptation, rises upward.

Secondly, we are to ask only as far as God allows us to ask. Even though He asks us to pour out our hearts (Ps. 62:8, 145:19), He does not aimlessly give us free rein to give into our silly and selfish impulses. When He promises to give Christians their request, His tolerance does not go so far as to give in to every single desire they have.

In both these instances, we often get it wrong, because not only do we call on God without humility or reverence, but we selfishly bring our own ambitions, whatever they are, before the throne of God. If we pray like this, we act foolishly. We would be embarrassed to act the same way with other people the way we arrogantly come to God.

That is why people in ancient days ended up turning to different gods for their different wishes: the ambitious looked to Jupiter; the greedy ones turned to Mercury; the educated went to Apollo and Minerva; the aggressive, Mars; the lustful, Venus. Today, it is the same when people who pray give in to their own improper desires. God's generosity and kindness are not to be mocked, and so He places our wishes under the restriction of His authority. This is why John said: "And this is the confidence that we have toward him, that if we ask anything according to his will he hears us" (1 John 5:14).

But since we fall so far from such perfection, we need to look for someone to help us. Just as the focus of our mind should be on God, so the desires of our hearts should follow the same direction. But we don't get it right, or we grow tired, or we get carried off on the wrong track. To help in this weakness, God gives us the guidance of the Spirit in our prayers to show us what is right and bring our emotions under control. "Likewise the Spirit helps us in our weakness. For we do not know what to pray for as we ought, but the Spirit himself intercedes for us with groanings too deep for words" (Rom. 8:26). Not that He actually prays or groans, but He motivates in us the desires and confidence that we naturally struggle to have.

There is a reason Paul uses the phrase "groanings too deep for words" to talk about the prayers that Christians make under the guidance of the Spirit. For those who are really trained in prayer are not unaware of the worries and cares that can hinder and block them so that they can hardly speak properly. It doesn't mean we can be lazy and leave all the praying to the Holy Spirit as our human nature so often wants to do. It doesn't mean we wait until He takes over our minds, but because we are tired of our own laziness, we become desperate for the Spirit's help. When Paul tells us to pray "in the Spirit" (1 Cor. 14:15), he does not mean that we should stop being alert. While the inspiration of the Spirit is able to form our prayers, He does not get in the way of our own efforts, since that is how God tests the faith in our hearts.

Daily Reflection

Having a notebook and pen will really help you, not only as you read each chapter, but to record verses and to write down your thoughts and answers in these reflections. Our minds can wander so fast that within a few minutes of having read a portion, we have forgotten it. It is good to write things down and revisit them. This jogs the memory but will also help to keep the ideas fresh in your mind so that they can begin to work themselves out in your thoughts as God shows you things.

1. Why does Calvin begin with keeping our minds focused in prayer?
2. How do you think lifting hands helps? Have you ever tried it?
3. How do we sometimes mock God's generosity?
4. Why do you think we need help in our praying, and how does the Holy Spirit help us?

26

THE HOLY SPIRIT'S HELP

Likewise the Spirit helps us in our weakness. For we do not know what to pray for as we ought, but the Spirit himself intercedes for us with groanings too deep for words. And he who searches hearts knows what is the mind of the Spirit.
—Rom. 8:26-7

"Likewise the Spirit helps us in our weakness." So that none of us can say that we are so weak and cannot bear so many heavy burdens, we are given the help of the Spirit, which is sufficient to overcome all difficulties. There is no more reason for any of us to complain that bearing the cross is beyond our own strength since we are sustained by a supernatural power. In the Greek, it means the Spirit takes on part of the burden so that He not only helps and comforts us but lifts us up as though He was under the burden with us. The word *"weakness"* is used to show that unless we are supported by God's hand, we are soon overwhelmed by many evils. Paul reminds us that even though we are weak in every way, and these threaten to make us fall, there is still sufficient protection in God's Spirit to keep us from falling and from being overwhelmed by so much evil. At the same time, these supplies of the Spirit prove to us that it is by God's appointment that we strive, by *"groanings,"* for our redemption.

"For we do not know what to pray for as we ought but the Spirit himself intercedes for us."

Paul had already spoken of the testimony of the Spirit, by which we know that God is our Father, and which allows us to dare call on Him as our Father. He now again refers to the second part, invocation, and says that we are taught by the same Spirit how to pray and what to ask for in our prayers. God does not bring suffering on us that we will feed on hidden grief, but that we can unburden ourselves by prayer, and exercise our faith.

There are many interpretations of this passage, but Paul is simply saying this: We are blind in the way we speak to God because as we sense the evil in us, our minds are more disturbed and confused in choosing what is correct and appropriate. For those who say that a format or rule for prayer is being prescribed to us in God's word, our thoughts continue to be burdened with darkness until the Spirit guides them by His light.

Even though it looks as if our prayers have not been heard by God, Paul concludes that His favor shines in the desire for prayer, because no one can have any holy or godly aspirations by themselves. The unbelievers do blab out their prayers, but they only play with God because there is nothing sincere or correct in them. The method to pray correctly must be suggested by the Spirit, and He calls those groanings into which we speak, for this reason—because they exceed the capability of our own minds. And the Spirit is said to intercede, not because He humbles Himself to pray or to groan, but because He stirs up in our hearts those desires which we should have. He also affects our hearts in such a way that these desires, in their passion, penetrate into heaven itself. And Paul acknowledges all of this to the grace of the Spirit. We are told to knock, but no one can premeditate even one syllable, except God by the secret impulse of His Spirit who knocks at our door and opens our hearts for Himself.

"And he who searches hearts knows what is the mind of the Spirit."

This is a remarkable reason for strengthening our confidence, that we are heard by God when we pray through His Spirit, for He knows our desires, even as the thoughts of His own Spirit. The use of the word *"knows"* is to show that God does not regard these emotions of the Spirit as new and strange, or that he rejects them as unreasonable, but that He allows them and accepts them. As already shown, God helps us when he draws us to Himself, so he adds another consolation —that our prayers, which He directs, will not end in disappointment. The reason is that He conforms us to His own will. We must also learn that what holds the first place in prayer is in line with the will of the Lord, who is not under obligation to our wishes. So, if we want our prayers to be acceptable to God, we must pray that He may regulate them according to His will.

Daily Reflection

Without the Spirit, our prayers become dead and lifeless. They are like difficult donkeys that we try to force this way and that. Not just prayer but understanding the Bible and God's ways, which also is very hard without the Helper. That is why the Holy Spirit came, to comfort, guide, and help us in our Christian walk.

1. Have you ever experienced the Holy Spirit in your prayers?
2. What do you think about talking/praying in tongues? Read 1 Corinthians 14.
3. What do you think it means to "groan" in prayer?
4. What reason do we have to strengthen our confidence?

27

PRAY IN THE SPIRIT

What am I to do? I will pray with my spirit, but I will pray with my mind also; I will sing praise with my spirit, but I will sing with my mind also. Otherwise, if you give thanks with your spirit...
—1 Cor. 14:15-16

To speak into the air is to beat the air for no reason (1 Cor. 9:26). Your voice will not reach God or man but will vanish into the air.

Paul says it is a big mistake if the mind is not focused in prayer. What else do we do in prayer, but pour out our thoughts and desires before God? Since prayer is the spiritual worship of God, how can it just come from the lips, and not from the inner soul? The devil has convinced people to believe that they are praying correctly if they just make their lips move. Some churches justify saying prayers without any understanding, even allowing uneducated people to mutter without reason.

"What am I to do? I will pray with my spirit."

Paul adds this in case anyone should ask, "Is the spirit useless in prayer?" He teaches us that it is acceptable to pray with the spirit, as long as the mind is active at the same time—the understanding. He says using a spiritual gift in prayer is good, but only if the mind is engaged.

Paul says, "If spiritual gifts are what you want, let them be for edification." Then you will know that you have attained an excellence that is true and praiseworthy—when you are an advantage to the church. But he does not give permission to anyone to desire an ambition to excel, even to the benefit of the church. Instead, he shows how short they come from what they pursue and lets them know who should be most highly esteemed. A person can be esteemed as much as they eagerly devote themselves to bringing edification. It is our part to have this one object in view—that the Lord may be exalted, and that His kingdom may be enlarged every day.

The term *"spirit,"* in this context, means spiritual gifts. We must remember what Paul stated previously, that it is one and the same Spirit, who gives to every person various gifts according to his will (1 Cor. 12:11).

When he says, *"I will sing praise,"* Paul uses this example instead of making a general statement. Just as the praises of God were the subject of the Psalms—blessing God, or giving thanks to Him—so, in our supplications, we either ask something from God, or we acknowledge some blessing that has been given us.

"Otherwise, if you give thanks with your spirit."

So far, Paul has been showing that our prayers will be useless and unfruitful if understanding does not accompany the voice. Now, he also speaks of public prayers. "If the person who says the prayers in the name of the people is not understood by the congregation, how will everyone add their desires, to take part in them? There is no fellowship in prayer unless everyone can unite in the same mind and attitude. This also applies to blessing or giving thanks to God."

In verse 16, Paul also gives the idea that one of the ministers said prayers, and that the whole congregation followed the words of that one person with their minds until he had finished, and then they all said "Amen" to agree that the prayer was one they all had in common. Amen is a Hebrew word that comes from the same term signifying faithfulness or truth. It is a sign of confirmation. The word was familiar among the Jews for many years before it made its way from them to the Gentiles, and the Greeks used it as if it was part of their own language. So, it came to be a term in common use among all nations.

Daily Reflection

Allowing room for the Holy Spirit to lead and guide you might be a foreign experience. It is not a spooky, weird phenomenon. It is ordered and practical for all Christians to be able to fully engage with God and everything He has for us. As you work through the chapters and reflections, remember to be still, wait, and listen. The Holy Spirit wants to teach and guide you.

1. What do you understand about the term *"spirit,"* used here by Paul?
2. How do you manage to engage with the mind and the spirit?
3. What is your understanding of spiritual gifts? Read 1 Corinthians 12.

28

JESUS PRAYED

In the days of his flesh, Jesus offered up prayers and supplications, with loud cries and tears, to him who was able to save him from death, and he was heard because of his reverence. Although he was a son, he learned obedience through what he suffered.
—Heb. 5:7, 8

Jesus looked for relief from the Father and was heard, yet still died, that he would come to obedience.

"*In the days of his flesh.*"

The writer of Hebrews is saying that the time of our hardships is limited. This is a huge encouragement, knowing there will be an end to our suffering.

1. Jesus was a Son, and yet He subjected Himself to suffering for our sake. Who of us could dare refuse the same condition?

2. Jesus looked for a way to be delivered from His temptations and hardships, so no one would think He was emotionless and felt nothing. If Jesus had known no sorrow, we would receive no comfort from His sufferings.

"With loud cries and tears."

We see the intensity of Jesus' grief when He prayed: "My Father, if it be possible, let this cup pass from me" (Matt. 26:42, Luke 22:42), and "My God, my God, why have you forsaken me?" (Matt. 27:46). It is clear that He was overwhelmed with real sorrow and desperately prayed for His Father's help. What can we learn from this? Whenever our hardships overwhelm us, we can remember the Son of God who struggled in the same way, and because He has gone before us, there is no reason for us to lose hope.

We are also reminded that deliverance can only be found in God, and what better guidance can we have in prayer than the example of Jesus? The writer says that He prayed *"to him who was able to save him from death"*; He went to God the only Deliverer. His tears and crying are evidence of this.

"And he was heard."

This is added in case we think Jesus' prayers were rejected because He was not immediately delivered from His struggles—God's mercy and help were always ready and available. So, we can conclude that God often hears our prayers, even when it is not evident to us. Even though we cannot prescribe to God, and He is not compelled to give us whatever requests we have in our minds or say with our mouths, yet He responds when it has to do with our salvation. When we seem to be apparently rejected, we gain far more than if He gave us all our requests.

But how was Jesus heard when He was afraid, as He faced the death that He feared? We must consider what it was He was afraid of: He only dreaded death because He saw in it the curse of God, and that He had to wrestle with the guilt of all iniquities, and also with hell itself. This was the reason for His anxiety because God's judgment was severe and unbearable. Then He received what he prayed for when he rose as a conqueror from the pains of death; when He was kept by the saving hand of the Father; when after a short struggle, He won a glorious victory over Satan, sin, and hell. We often ask for this and that but without the correct intentions, and still God comforts us even though He does not give us what we ask for.

"He learned obedience."

The reason for Jesus' sufferings was to be accustomed to obedience; not that he was forced to do so, or that He needed to be trained as horses have to be tamed, because He was totally willing to give His Father the obedience He deserved. This was done for our benefit that He would be an example of submission—even to death. We could even say that by His death, Jesus learned what it was to obey God since He was led in a special way to deny Himself. In renouncing His own will, He gave Himself over to His Father so that He would willingly go through the death He dreaded. This means Jesus, through His sufferings, taught us how far we need to go to submit to and obey God.

Daily Reflection

The best model we have of anything related to our Christianity is always Jesus. He walked, lived, spoke, breathed, and was tempted as we are. Yet, He led a completely righteous life, given and surrendered to the Father. That is what we aspire to, to be more Christ-like. Learning to pray is best done by following His example, and the writer of Hebrews gives us a good insight into that here.

1. Do you ever have intensity in your prayers?
2. Why is it hard for Christians when we do not receive what we pray for?
3. How does this teach us obedience?

29

PRAYING PUBLICLY

And when you pray, you must not be like the hypocrites. For they love to stand and pray in the synagogues and at the street corners, that they may be seen by others.... But when you pray, go into your room and shut the door and pray to your Father who is in secret. And your Father who sees in secret will reward you.... Do not heap up empty phrases as the Gentiles do.
—Matt. 6:5-7

Everything in the church "should be done decently and in order" as Paul says (1 Cor. 14:40).

This is why Jesus warned against *"empty phrases"* (Matt. 6:7). He did not say we could have long prayers, or pray frequently, or with lots of passion, but warned against thinking we can get anything from God by harassing Him with lots of extravagant chatter, as if He could be persuaded to do what we wanted. We know that hypocrites who are not really thinking of God when they pray, arrogantly offer up their prayers as if they were part of a show. The Pharisee, who thanked God that he was not like other men, proclaimed his praises before men as if wanted to build a reputation for holiness through his prayers (Luke 18:11). *"Empty phrases,"* uselessly repeating the same shallow prayers, and using long phrases for the show are all just a mockery of God. Therefore, it is not strange that it should not be done in the church, so every feeling that is expressed is sincere, from the heart.

Another thing Jesus criticizes is when hypocrites pray for the attention of others (Matt. 6:5). The true goal of prayer is to carry our thoughts directly to God. Whether we praise Him or ask for help, He is still the main focus of our minds and hearts. Prayer is an overflow of our feelings for God, the searcher of hearts (Rom. 8:27).

This is why Jesus made the rule: *"When you pray, go into your room and shut the door and pray to your Father who is in secret. And your Father who sees in secret will reward you"* (Matt. 6:6).

Using the example of hypocrites who wanted praise from people for their eloquent prayers, He gave a better option— *"go into your room and shut the door and pray."* In this way, He taught us to find a place where we can turn all our thoughts inwards and enter deeply into our hearts, promising that God will communicate with the feelings of our mind, which is part of our body's temple (2 Cor. 6:16).

He did not mean we cannot pray in other places also, but He showed that prayer is of a secret nature, where the mind needs quiet, away from the busy interruptions of the day. So, even Jesus, when He wanted to go deeper in prayer, withdrew to a quiet place away from the bustle of the world. His example reminds us not to neglect this method which helps the mind that is prone to wander.

But Jesus never refrained from prayer just because He was in the middle of a crowd, so we must also "pray, lifting holy hands" whenever there is a need in all places (1 Tim. 2:8). So, anyone who will not pray in the presence of other Christians does not really know what it is to pray alone, on their own. In the same way, anyone who neglects to pray alone and in private, regardless of how often they attend prayer meetings or services, prays to the wind because they submit more to the opinion of people than to the secret judgment of God.

So there is no question about the validity of prayers in church, Jesus showed their importance when He called the temple the "house of prayer" (Isa. 56:7; Matt. 21:13). Using this expression, He showed that the duty of prayer is a main part of His worship, and for Christians to be able to do so in unity, His temple becomes a covering banner. A promise was also added, "Praise is due to you, O God, in Zion, and to you shall vows be performed" (Psalm 65:1). By these words, the Psalmist reminds us that the prayers of the church are never in vain because God always gives His people a reason to sing with joy. Even though the Old Covenant has passed, because God was pleased by the unity of faith in prayer, there is no doubt that the same promise still belongs to us—a promise that Jesus endorsed and that Paul declares to be true and active.

Since God instructs us in the Bible to engage in corporate prayer, churches are where this happens. So, anyone who refuses to join Christians in this have no argument that being in their room is enough to obey the command of the Lord. Because God promises to give to those two or three gathered in His name whatever they ask (Matt. 18:19-20), He shows that He is not against public prayer as long as there is no pretending or looking for praise from people, and provided there is a true and sincere desire in the heart. And just because churches are the place for public prayer, we should not believe that God lives there and listens more to us there, making the building or the prayers holier than they are.

Since *we* are the true temples of God, we must pray in ourselves if we want to approach God in His holy temple. We have a command to pray without distinction of place, "in spirit and in truth" (John 4:23). It is true that God ordered the temple to be the dedicated place to offer prayers and sacrifices, but this was at a time when the truth was not yet revealed. Even the temple of the Jews could not confine the presence of God within its walls but was there to train them to think and meditate on the image of the true temple. So, severe criticism was given by Isaiah and Stephen to those who thought that God could live in temples made with hands (Isa. 66:2; Acts 7:48).

Daily Reflection

Some people enjoy public praying, others not so much. We are all called to pray in our personal relationships with Jesus, but there are also times when collective prayer is necessary and encouraging. Prayer meetings, church services, and other times call for prayer to be said aloud for everyone to hear and agree.

1. Calvin makes a bold statement that anyone who won't pray amongst Christians does not know about praying on their own. Do you agree?
2. Do you find it easy or difficult to pray in the midst of others?
3. What important distinction is there between the church building and us as "temples"?

30

DANIEL'S EXAMPLE (PART ONE)

O Lord, hear; O Lord, forgive. O Lord, pay attention and act. Delay not, for your own sake, O my God, because your city and your people are called by your name.
—Dan. 9:19

Daniel does not use big, eloquent words as hypocrites do, but simply teaches by his example the true way to pray. He says, *"O Lord, hear."* Since God seemed to be deaf to all the prayers of the people, Daniel begged Him to turn His ear. Next, he adds, *"O Lord, pay attention."* When God neglected to answer, it must have dashed the hopes of the believers, because the Israelites were treated so badly. They were oppressed and suffered terrible misfortune in everything else. Yet God passed by all these troubles of His people as if his eyes were shut. For this reason, Daniel now asks Him to open his eyes.

Our prayers should continue in the midst of hardship. When God pushes us to the edge, we should be even more persistent, because this affliction is there to wake us up from our laziness. That is why it says, "Therefore let everyone who is godly offer prayer to you at a time when you may be found" (Ps. 32:6). Our opportunity comes when we are overwhelmed by circumstances, because then God stirs us up and corrects our lethargy. Let us learn, therefore, to become violent and zealous in prayer whenever God urges and incites us in this way.

Repentance and faith should be united in our prayers. But repentance throws people down, and faith raises them up again. At first, these two ideas seem opposite to each other, but it is not possible to raise our prayers and vows to heaven without pushing them to the lowest depths. When a sinner comes into the presence of God, he must fall completely down. This is the genuine effect of repentance. This is why Christians cast down all their prayers, whenever they acknowledge they are unworthy of the Almighty's attention.

Jesus gives us a picture of this through the tax collector, who beats his chest and begs for forgiveness with a dejected expression (Luke 18:13). So, we throw down our prayers in that spirit of humility that comes from penitence. Then we lift our prayers by faith because when God invites us to Himself and shows us His generosity and favor, we raise ourselves up. Daniel's prayer also shows that God hears prayer, as we read in Psalm 65:2. When we see God is generous to us, we boldly approach His presence and pray with confidence knowing He is pleased with the sacrifice which we offer.

Daniel does not display his eloquence, as hypocrites usually do, but simply teaches by his example the true law and method of prayer. He was driven by a focused passion for the purpose of drawing others with him. God, therefore, worked in him by His Spirit to use him so his prayer became an example to the whole church. He calls the people together to witness his zeal and passion, inviting them to follow his example as coming from God, not himself.

"O Lord, hear."

Daniel implies that God's deafness was intentional because He was angry with the people. We sometimes foolishly wonder why God does not answer our prayers as soon as it comes from our lips. But we see that God takes His time because we are cold and dull, and our sins are an obstacle between ourselves and His ear.

"O Lord, pay attention and act."

Daniel admits the people had provoked God's anger for a long time, but they were unworthily oppressed by cruel enemies, and that this severe hardship should be enough for God to have pity on them.

"Delay not, for your own sake, O my God."

Seventy years had already passed away since God had formally exiled His people and had refused to be generous toward them.

The practical lesson here is that it is impossible to pray properly unless we rise above whatever comes against us. If we measure God's favor according to our own circumstances, we will lose the desire to pray—we will be worn down by our hardships and be totally unable to lift our minds up to God. Whenever God seems to have delayed for a long time, He must be constantly begged not to delay.

He adds *"… for your own sake, O my God,"* removing any confidence that hypocrites think they have that can gain God's favor. He confirms that it is not for our sake when the verse continues:

"Because your city and your people are called by your name."

Daniel begins to show us that his prayers were not useless and unproductive, because Gabriel was sent to encourage him.

We should not think that God ignores our prayers because others seem to pray with more passion and sincerity. If we compare ourselves with Daniel's praying, we are definitely far behind him.

We can be confident that our prayers will never be in vain. Even if our prayers are not as passionate as his, God will still listen to them, so long as they are based on faith and repentance. That is why he said, "While I was speaking and praying, confessing my sin and the sin of my people Israel" (Dan. 9:20).

Through Daniel, the Holy Spirit made it clear that God's grace is available to every sinner who comes and begs for it. Daniel shows why we do not receive help when we ask for it: Our hardships cause us to complain, and yet we never look up to God, where our help and comfort come from. So, he encourages us to pray by saying his requests were heard.

This encourages us to pray because if we seek God as a deliverer our prayers will never be in vain or be unfruitful. Those who have true faith and repentance, even a small amount, will never bring their prayers to God in vain.

Daily Reflection

Daniel was a prophet and a man of prayer. One of the most famous stories about him recounts lions in the den. After refusing to bow down to idols, he chooses to pray to God. His defiance results in a miraculous turnaround where the Lord spares his life. Who better to learn about prayer than from someone who put it so highly on his priorities that he was willing to be put to death for it? In this instance, his reputation has been restored, and he stands as the prophet who stands in the gap for the Israelites.

1. What do you think about the way Daniel begins his prayer here?
2. Have you ever prayed on behalf of others?
3. What does Calvin mean about it being impossible to pray unless we rise above circumstances?

31

DANIEL'S EXAMPLE (PART TWO)

While I was speaking and praying, confessing my sin and the sin of my people Israel, and presenting my plea before the Lord my God for the holy hill of my God...
—Dan. 9:20

Daniel shows us what is necessary for finding God's favor: We should anticipate His judgment by condemning ourselves. Daniel says that he confessed his sin and that of the Israelites. He does not mention one specific sin but includes every kind of evil. It is as if, when he was confessing his own sinfulness, he confessed on behalf of all the people as well. He was guilty, without the slightest hope of forgiveness, unless God, whom they had offended, was gracious enough to reconcile them to Himself.

In Ezekiel 14:14, God names the three most perfect people who had lived, and Daniel is one of them. But even Daniel confesses that he is a sinner before God, and completely rejects his own righteousness, openly stating that his only hope of salvation is in the mercy of God. Augustine often used this passage to show that there is no one in the world who does not need God's mercy. If there had been such a person, then the Lord, who is the only one to judge, could have found him. But He says His servant Daniel is one of the most perfect, if only three are chosen since the beginning of history.

But Daniel puts himself in the same category as sinners, without any false humility, but with a clear conscience before God. He is not pretending or being a hypocrite, because those who claim to be perfect are nothing more than evil in spirit. Therefore, we must hold on to this principle: no man, even if partly angelic, can approach God, unless he finds favor by sincere and simple confession of his sins. He is as good as a criminal before God. So, this is our righteousness —to confess that we are guilty so God may graciously forgive us.

We can see the same instructions in the words of Jesus: "Forgive us our debts [trespasses, sins]" (Matt. 6:12; Luke 11:4.) Who did He intend this prayer for? Surely it was for all His disciples, all His followers. If anyone thinks that they do not need this example of prayer which contains this confession of sin, then they should rather leave the school of Christ, and go somewhere else!

Next Daniel adds, "... *for the holy hill of my God.*"

This is another reason he gives for being heard by God: It is his concern for the good and safety of the church. If we only look at our own interests and do not care about our neighbors or fellow brothers, then we are not worthy to get anything from God. But, if we want our prayers to be pleasing to God, and to produce useful fruit, then we need to learn to unite the whole body of the church with us, and not only to think about what is good for ourselves but what will help all God's chosen people.

He continues and says, *"While I was speaking in prayer."*

It seems that Daniel was not only praying emotionally and inwardly but also aloud for others to hear. Often this can mean praying in thought, when a person does not use their mouth but thinks their prayers in their head. But here, it sounds as if Daniel had suddenly started speaking aloud, as he became more passionate and enthusiastic in prayer. There is another reason that most Christians tend to pray in their minds: we are naturally slow, and only after the thought, do our mouths begin to speak. That is why Daniel began his prayers silently and mentally but was also able to say them verbally and aloud.

It is clear that we can get nothing by our prayers without God's previously deciding to give it to us it. This is not a contradiction. It says, "He fulfills the desire of those who fear him," and yet He does what He had determined before the creation of the world (Ps. 145:19).

He had predicted the end of the people's exile through Jeremiah (Jer. 25:11). Daniel already knew this but did not stop from praying because he knew that God's promises do not give us room to be lazy or complacent. So, he prayed, and

God showed how his desires were not in vain as they concerned the welfare of the church.

"At the beginning of your pleas for mercy a word went out."

As soon as Daniel began to pray, he was divinely answered. When we become anxious and depressed because our prayers seem to have no effect, and because we want immediate answers, we must look at Daniel. He was approved by God but was only answered after a long time, without being allowed to see it with his own eyes. He died in exile and never lived to see any of his prophecies come true.

Daily Reflection

This last part of looking at Daniel's prayer has some very interesting points. Looking at them, Calvin brings up some concepts that can open our eyes to understanding how we should approach prayer if we want them to be powerful and effective.

1. What is necessary for finding God's favor?
2. Is confession a part of your prayer time with God?
3. Having read through the book and worked through these reflections, how would you rate your prayer life now? Has there been any growth?

If you are inspired and challenged to go deeper and further in your prayer life, then there are other books written by godly men that are worth looking at. These men, just like John Calvin, did not just write or speak about prayer, it was an integral part of their lives.

- *John Bunyan On Prayer*
- *Matthew Henry On Prayer*
- *How to Pray Effectively* by R.A. Torrey
- *The Power of Prayer* by Charles Spurgeon

ABOUT JOHN CALVIN

Growing up during the Reformation, John Calvin found himself at the center of a religious dispute between the dominant Catholic Church and those seeking to return to the gospel. For a man as timid and sometimes weak-willed as he was, his role as one of the foremost campaigners for truth is even more remarkable.

Born in 1509, a few miles outside of Paris, Calvin received the best education possible through a private tutor and then went on to study theology, where he graduated at the very young age of 17. However, his father decided he should rather follow a career in law. Calvin learned Greek and honed his skills of rhetoric and analysis, which would serve him well in his study and defense of the Bible.

After his father's death, Calvin found some freedom and continued his own studies, even coming across Martin Luther's works. Around this time, he was born again and his path to becoming one of the most prolific stalwarts of the Bible began. In 1533, he escaped from Paris, being lowered down from a window by sheets, and later had to leave France altogether when religious authorities withstood his activism.

His time in exile allowed him to publish one of his most well-known works, *The Institutes of the Christian Religion*, a manuscript that officially pitched him against the Catholics. Outlining the basics of Christianity, it would later be used by those following Calvinistic ideals. While in Geneva, he was persuaded to stay and took up the role of minister; however, his vision of bring order to the church there made him plenty of enemies, and once again, he found himself being forced out.

In Germany, he married, and although it was a happy union, none of their children survived. His wife, Idelette Bure, passed away in 1549 after being with Calvin for nine years. He never remarried. During this time, he was recalled to Geneva to bring moral and civil order to the city, even though he had been banished once before for attempting to do just that!

The first decade was an intense time of struggle as he pushed for reform. Openly confronted by a group called the Libertines, he faced countless threats. But Calvin was persistent, and by 1555, the tide turned. His opposition has ended, and a huge change came over the city as a result of him preaching the Word week in and week out.

By this time, his influence had reached France, England, and Scotland, and even Martin Luther. John Knox visited his church and commented that it was like being in the "days of the apostles." Setting up an Academy to teach theology, Calvin had over a thousand students, many of whom would suffer and die as martyrs for their stance as Christians.

From his early thirties, Calvin began to experience health issues, ranging from stomach pain to migraines. His worst illness came in 1558 when he contracted a severe fever. From then on, he often coughed blood because of the strain on his voice from preaching. Tired and frail, he gave his last sermon in 1564 in Geneva, and just over three months later, at the age of 54, he died.

Dedicated and thorough, Calvin's stand for the truth of God's Word become one of the pivotal moments in church history. His relentless pursuit of sound doctrine may have been unpopular with those in authority at the time, but it opened the way for countless Christians to find freedom and grace in Jesus.

BIBLIOGRAPHY

Calvin, J. (1999). *Calvin's commentaries*. Baker Book House.
Calvin, J. (2020). *Prayer: The chief exercise of faith*. (D. Benge, Ed.). H&E Publishing.
Crossway. (2001). *English standard version Bible*. Crossway Bibles.

www.ingramcontent.com/pod-product-compliance
Lightning Source LLC
LaVergne TN
LVHW020424070526
838199LV00003B/272